joy in the journey

anita pearce

forever books
WINNIPEG, CANADA
www.foreverbooks.ca

Cover Design: Yvonne Parks Design
Book Design: Andrew Mackay
Managing Editor: Rick Johnson
Printed in Canada
Published by:

Forever Books

WINNIPEG CANADA
www.foreverbooks.ca

Dedicated to
Velma Henderson,
my sister and my friend.
I deeply love and admire you.

Acknowledgements

God has blessed me with friends and colleagues who continually challenge me to excellence. I am profoundly grateful to many people who have provided invaluable assistance in producing this book.

I wish to express particular appreciation to:

Alice Dutcyvich, for your meticulous attention to detail during the hours spent going over the manuscript. Your enthusiasm for grammar is astonishing; your patience in advising me is amazing! Your friendship is a treasure.

Doreen Holdsworth, for your willingness to share your expertise. You are a gifted proofreader. I am deeply grateful for your proficiency.

Darlene Kienle, for your faithful friendship. Your continuing support is an encouragement to me. Your passion for Christ and for life is an inspiration to me.

The board of Inspiration Ministries, for encouraging me to continue to write books for the glory of God and the furtherance of His Kingdom.

Table of Contents

Introduction

The backpack was ready. There was fresh coffee in the thermos, sandwiches and cookies in the bag, a blanket to sit on. There were wieners and buns for a wiener roast, some dry wood, matches, an axe, and a knife. My anticipation of adventure had kept me awake a good part of the night. My mind carefully re-calculated the supplies my friend and I would need for a hike and a picnic. Finally we were on our way.

I was already envisioning our arrival at the destination. The smell of the coffee and expectation of lunch made me want to hurry. The abundance of mosquitoes irritated me, and I kept an anxious eye on the sky in case a rain cloud would appear. My friend however, older and wiser, kept stopping on the path. A flower here, a bug there, a hidden bird's nest—fascinating details kept attracting her attention.

We didn't make high-speed progress, but what priceless lessons I learned. We discussed the beauty of wild flowers. We watched unidentified bugs scuttle along a branch. We inspected the bird's nest. A startled doe and her fawn bounced away through the tall grass. Countless intriguing delights were discovered. The steep, rough path seemed almost insignificant in light of our enjoyment.

Soon enough, we laid out the blanket and spread the picnic. In retrospect, the greatest thrill of the day was not the arrival at our destination but the exploration and discovery of unexpected marvels along the way. Someone has stated, "A truly happy person is one who can enjoy the scenery on a detour."

As we hurry and worry along the path of life we often overlook or bypass the greatest treasures and possibilities. The Lord can reveal His glory along the road if we let Him. He can teach us to discover hope in hardship, beauty in ashes, and joy in the journey.

Chapter One

INFLUENTIAL IMPACT

We must never underestimate the effect we have on others whose paths we cross on the road of life. There are people who will be forever changed because we have met with them. The words we say, the attitudes we express, and the actions we display will leave an influence long after we walk on. A smile here or a kind word there may make an eternal difference in someone we meet.

May we take advantage of every opportunity to plant the seeds of faith and good will, to be ambassadors of Christ, and examples of His grace. Part of the peace prayer of Saint Francis of Assisi states:

Make me a channel of your peace,
Where there is despair, let me bring hope;
Where there is darkness, only light;
And where there is sadness, ever joy.

In Acts Chapter 9, a few believers gathered on the city wall in the darkness to assist Saul of Tarsus in his escape from Damascus. This former murderer of Christians had been powerfully transformed when he was converted to Christ a brief time before. The infuriated religious elite now sought his life.

As the huddled group put Saul in a basket and gingerly let him down over the wall they had no way of knowing the far-reaching impact of their actions. They did not know that this man would become the Apostle Paul. They could not have imagined that one day he would preach the gospel across Europe and Asia. None could foresee that the Holy Spirit would inspire Paul to become the author of nearly half the New Testament, or that his influence would affect the entire world.

On that night so long ago, those believers only saw a fellow Christian in distress. They made themselves available to hold the rope—a simple action that changed the world. We must never underestimate the impact of our words, attitudes, or actions. We also can hold ropes for others and leave an eternal legacy.

For want of a nail the shoe was lost.
For want of a shoe the horse was lost.
For want of a horse the rider was lost.
For want of a rider the battle was lost.
For want of a battle the kingdom was lost.
And all for the want of a horseshoe nail.
— English Nursery Rhyme

I have always enjoyed speaking in public—in private too, for that matter! By the time I started third grade I had already won a number of awards in speaking contests. I might add that I had also earned a number of other experiences for talking when I should have kept quiet!

As a teenager, I had the assurance that one day it would be God's will for me to minister His Word. The insecurities of adolescence, however, brought questions and uncertainties as I searched for acceptance, direction, and confirmed purpose. Family and friends spoke words of encouragement that helped clarify my path. I was profoundly blessed by the godly influences surrounding me. Dozens of individuals marked my life for good. By observing some people, I also learned huge life lessons of what *not* to do.

When I was about sixteen years of age, together with my classmates, I was to prepare and deliver a speech for the English class. I was passionate about the subject. It was a challenge to me and the other students to consider eternal values as we faced the future. The speech would eventually grant me opportunity to compete at a provincial level. However, in that classroom in front of my friends, I was not only passionate, but also *terrified!* I returned to my place feeling totally inadequate.

"Very well done," the teacher acknowledged. It was only three words, which were actually spoken rather casually, but I heard them—and they changed my life! Then she added, "I understand you intend to go into the ministry. For heaven's sake, you will have to learn to be less enthusiastic. Everyone knows most people go to church to sleep; no one will have an opportunity to sleep while you speak!"

While Apostle Paul was preaching in the city of Ephesus, a certain silversmith became concerned about the loss of revenue from the sale of his silver shrines. He created a rumor that Paul's preaching would destroy the worship of the goddess Diana. The rumor turned into a riot and the whole city was in an uproar. In Acts 19:32, we find an interesting phrase:

"The assembly was in confusion: Some were shouting one thing, some another. Most of the people did not even know why they were there" (NIV).

It was the classic example of the mob effect—people being swept along in the emotion of the moment without any idea of fundamental reasons. There are people today who are easily influenced by misinformation. They jump to conclusions without carefully analyzing the facts.

In our society, where media constantly bombards our senses, we need to be *re-sensitized* to seek the truth. We must not be easily led by those who would manipulate us, attempting to accomplish their ulterior purposes. We need God's wisdom in choosing what influences our thoughts, words, and actions.

Some minds are like concrete:
thoroughly mixed up and permanently set.
— Author Unknown

An acquaintance had taken her five-year-old granddaughter shopping for a new pair of rubber boots. Proudly sporting her new floral-designed footwear, she and her grandmother used the elevator to exit the building. First a man, then another woman joined them in the elevator. They descended one floor. The door opened. As the woman was leaving, however, she turned and sarcastically said to the man, "You need help: you're sick!" The astonished stranger was stunned by the woman's outburst.

On the next floor, the grandmother and granddaughter left the elevator. The grandmother whispered, "I didn't like that woman. She wasn't very nice to that man."

"No, I didn't like her either," articulated the little girl, "she was standing on my new boots so I pinched her bottom!"

Some things are not as they seem. Often we make rapid assumptions and draw false conclusions. In reality, the situation may be very different than what we see from our limited perspective. It is easy to be influenced by our perceptions, which may not always be accurate. How surprising it can be when we get the full picture.

The Book of Esther is a beautiful story of God's intervention in a dangerous situation. One of the most startling realizations is that the Lord did not do it alone, but involved ordinary individuals. He equipped them with extraordinary courage to confront evil and be influences for righteousness—even at the risk of their own lives.

As Esther and her cousin Mordecai dared to be available as instruments in God's hand, doing what they could, the Lord intervened to do what they could not. The Lord only requires our willing co-operation.

There are three kinds of people:
Those who make things happen,
those who watch things happen,
and those who have no idea what happened.
— Author Unknown

Vaguely, through the haze of drowsiness that enveloped me, I could hear the irritating buzz—droning louder and louder. Then it stopped. I bolted, wide awake. Mosquito attack! I flapped my hand in the general direction of the last hum. Then it was: listen, buzz, slap, listen, buzz, slap.

Finally, in total exasperation, I got out of bed and turned on the light. As stealthily as any big game hunter, my eyes darted from corner to corner. One step, two steps, slap, buzz, search, one step, two step, slap. Success! One mosquito squished on the wall.

Someone once said, "If you ever wonder if small things can have an impact on your world, just try sleeping in a room with one live mosquito."

Often, we may feel our influence is insignificant, or our power to change our world is of little importance. However, as a small pebble thrown into a pool can create ripples extending across the entire surface, the effect of our lives may reach farther than we are able to imagine. We have the opportunity to spread kindness and encouragement to everyone we meet.

We read these words in Luke 6:36 to 38:

"Be merciful, just as your Father is merciful. Do not judge, and you will not be judged. Do not condemn, and you will not be condemned. Forgive, and you will be forgiven. Give, and it will be given to you. A good measure, pressed down, shaken together and running over, will be poured into your lap. For with the measure you use, it will be measured to you"
(NIV).

The universal principle of sowing and reaping applies to the spiritual world as well as the natural. It is an obvious fact that seed sown will produce multiples of the same type of plant. Jesus related this to the eternal virtues of mercy and judgment. He also made it clear that the harvest would be much more abundant than the sowing—this applies to both good and evil planting. How careful we must be, knowing the time of harvest shall surely come.

Watch your thoughts; they become words.
Watch your words; they become actions.
Watch your actions; they become habits.
Watch your habits; they become character.
Watch your character; it becomes your destiny.
— Author Unknown

I was walking alone along a city street when I saw a large man with a rather unkempt appearance approaching. Knowing I would pass near him, I immediately became wary and watchful. He stopped and was looking intently across the street. I didn't take my eyes off of him to see where he was looking. However, in my peripheral vision I detected a blind man approaching with his guide[1] dog. I nervously watched to see what would happen. To my utter astonishment, the rough, ragged stranger reached out to the blind man, offering to help him across the street.

I experienced an instant paradigm shift. As I continued walking down the street, I acknowledged that I have often quickly drawn conclusions about others based on my assumptions. I had suspected the unkempt stranger of suspicious character when actually his motives were kinder than mine. It is true that we often judge others by their actions but ourselves by our intentions.

Reality jolted me—I had bypassed opportunities to extend kindness because of personal prejudices or perceived intentions. On many occasions, others could have been encouraged or helped if I had been more sensitive.

I recently read an article stating that, during an average lifetime, a person affects about 10,000 people. Often, we are not conscious of the influence of our presence, personality, or performance.

The Apostle Paul probably never dreamed that his testimony and adventures while following Christ would affect all of Christendom for 2000 years. Our financial status and earthly success are temporal and fleeting. However, the impact of our life for Christ will last for eternity.

Setting an example is not the main means of influencing another; it is the only means.

— Albert Einstein

The flight had been delayed for technical reasons; cranky passengers were pushing in their rush to board the aircraft. The agents at the ticket counter were hard-pressed to maintain order; a number of passengers were caustic in their criticism. As I approached to board the plane I noticed that the stress was taking its toll on the attendant. His hands were visibly shaking as he processed my ticket.

Suddenly, I was prompted to say, "You are doing a very good job." He looked at me with astonishment as tears filled his eyes.

Pressed by the crowd behind, I had to move ahead quickly. As I found my seat, I couldn't help wondering at the deep impact a word of encouragement could make. Let us take every opportunity to speak uplifting words of kindness to all who cross our path.

The Jewish people had been permitted to return to Israel after seventy years of captivity in Babylon. Under the leadership of the governor, Nehemiah, they had begun to rebuild the walls of their ancient city. They completed this remarkable feat in fifty-two days. One of the keys to this phenomenal achievement can be discovered in Nehemiah 4:6:

"So built we the wall; and all the wall was joined together unto the half thereof: for the people had a mind to work."

Every individual is important and each contribution to a cause is of great value. However, when many work together with one mind, the accomplishments can be multiplied.

Working together is essential for success; even freckles would make a nice tan if they would get together.

— Author Unknown

No one knows what started the fire. As a result of severe drought conditions in my home province of Saskatchewan, the grass and fields, yellow and withered, were tinder dry. Reflected heat from broken glass, an accidental spark, or a lit match was all that was needed.

Suddenly, the sleepy little pasture at the end of our village burst into a roaring conflagration. Fanned by strong winds, the fire leaped the railroad tracks, then the highway, and was rapidly rolling across a parched stubble field, expanding by the second into a full-blown prairie fire.

From everywhere they came. Men picked up shovels, drove tractors, carried water. Women chased the cattle to safety. Passersby stopped to offer assistance. Within minutes over half the village was involved. Before the fire department even arrived, the fire was under control. As the result of fast thinking, excellent co-operation, willing effort, and common need, great disaster was averted.

As believers, we can make an immense difference by working together. The impact of our co-operation with Christ and one another can produce eternal results in transformed lives and destinies. Let's pull together in every circumstance—to pray, to give, and to do whatever God requires.

An old adage says, "Beauty is only skin deep." There is truth in this phrase. Whether we are contemplating houses or horses, people or places, cars or Christians, the most important qualities are those that cannot be seen at first glance. When a crisis comes, we need the enduring qualities of Christ's character to withstand the pressure.

Character is the result of consistently making positive choices that build righteous habits in our lives. When we are born again, we receive a new nature that desires to manifest God's will in our actions and attitudes. The Lord empowers us as we live out the principles of His Word. However, it is our daily decisions of right action that ultimately release God's power to grow beautiful character.

People are like stained-glass windows.
They sparkle and shine when the sun is out,
but when the darkness sets in,
their true beauty is revealed
only if there is a light within.
— Elisabeth Kubler-Ross

The shopping bug had bitten. However, when I tried on my purchase later, I discovered it was the wrong size. I took it back to the store but, to my consternation, I was told no refunds were given, only credits toward another purchase. I did not say anything but my expression showed my dismay and irritation. Another purchase was finally made.

As I left the shop, feeling quite annoyed, I thought of uncomplimentary comments I could have made. I was irritated with the owners of the store for not warning me of their refund policy. My sour thoughts were reflected in my hasty exit.

That evening in the service, not one, but *two* women approached me. They told me how excited they were that I had shopped in the store where they worked. They had both been too shy to approach me, but had told all of their workmates that I was the special Canadian evangelist who was speaking at their church!

I was greatly humbled and repented on the spot. How grateful I was that the Lord had helped me to keep my mouth shut, but how sad I felt that I had lost a precious opportunity to shine the love of Christ in an annoying situation. Often we miss the occasion to be an eternal blessing because of petty pouts over unimportant issues.

Much of the New Testament consists of letters written to the first-century believers. These epistles are filled with practical instructions on how Christians should live—revealing the character of Christ in day-by-day life.

The verses of Ephesians 4:29 to 32 contain an excellent example of Holy Spirit inspired advice for us to apply in our lives. Paul exhorts:

"Do not let any unwholesome talk come out of your mouths, but only what is helpful for building others up according to their needs, that it may benefit those who listen... Get rid of all bitterness, rage and anger, brawling and slander, along with every form of malice. Be kind and compassionate to one another, forgiving each other, just as in Christ God forgave you" (NIV).

Be kinder than necessary. Everyone is fighting some kind of battle.
— Author Unknown

It is easy to be consumed with our life situations and overlook our own faults, as well as the needs of others. However, from an open and repentant heart we can find fulfilment and often discover solutions. I read this *Prayer of a Seventeenth Century Nun,* written on a decorative tablecloth in France. The brutal honesty of this precious soul is both revealing and relevant.

Lord, Thou knowest better than I know myself that I am growing older and will someday be old. Keep me from the fatal habit of thinking that I must say something on every subject and on every occasion. Release me from craving to straighten out somebody's affairs. Make me thoughtful but not moody; helpful but not bossy. With my vast store of wisdom, it seems a pity not to use it all, but Thou knowest, Lord, that I want a few friends at the end.

Keep my mind free from the recital of endless details; give me wings to get to the point. Seal my lips upon my aches and pains. They are increasing and the love of rehearsing them is becoming sweeter as the years go by. I dare not ask for grace enough to enjoy the tales of other's pains, but help me to endure them with patience. I dare not ask for improved memory, but a growing humility and a lessening cocksureness when my memory seems to clash with the memories of others. Teach me the glorious lesson that occasionally, I may be mistaken.

Keep me reasonably sweet; I do not want to be a saint—some of them are so hard to live with—but a sour old person is one of the crowning works of the devil. Give me the ability to see good things in unexpected places, and talents in unexpected people. And give me, Lord, the grace to tell them so.

Chapter Two

GROWING IN GRATEFULNESS

Someone has said that if you want to look young, stand beside people who are older; if you wish to appear slimmer, stand near those who are heavier. When we are confronted with difficult circumstances, it is wise to consider others who may have greater afflictions than we do. When we count our blessings and choose an attitude of gratitude, our entire perspective can be transformed.

There are those who have made a habit of complaining. They have enveloped themselves with their own woes, forever oozing self-pity and negativism. We can choose to make a difference. When we reach out to the Lord and others, we discover the joy that deep gratitude can bring.

Every season has its beauty and charm, as well as its difficulties. In spring, the new leaves and flowers are preceded by mud and rainy days. In summer, along with the sunshine and warmth, there are those pesky mosquitoes. In autumn, the magnificent kaleidoscope of colored leaves soon falls and needs to be raked. The winter brilliance of fresh-fallen snow means frosty days, storms, and icy roads.

Life is a continuous changing of seasons. Let us learn to be grateful. Do not be dismayed by the obstacles. Soon enough, each season shall pass. Seek for the beauty and find joy in the journey.

When someone says, "Life is hard!" ask them, "Compared to what?"

— Author Unknown

We will probably never know what caused the food poisoning, but our digestive systems were in full revolt. The four of us, who shared the same apartment, spent most of one night and day beating a path to and from the bathroom. Being sick in a foreign country is never any fun but, in this particular developing[2] country where living conditions were rudimentary and poverty was prevalent, it was even less fun.

A grateful attitude can be learned; adversity can quickly reveal the truest priorities of life. Upon reflection, I was never so grateful for toilet paper, a toilet that worked, and for friends with whom to share misery. In the darkest moments, I was gloomily grateful that my "last will and testament" was in order!

In the crises of life, our priorities are readjusted. We realize that "the most important things in life aren't things." Our relationship with the Lord, our family, our friends, and good health, are precious treasures.

Although it may not be suitable to be thankful *for every* situation we experience, the scripture teaches us that we can maintain a grateful attitude *in* every trial. We are told in 1 Thessalonians 5:18:

"In everything give thanks: for this is the will of God in Christ Jesus concerning you."

By choosing to focus on the blessings rather than the difficulties, our entire demeanor can be transformed. Instead of being overwhelmed by the impossibilities, we find new strength flowing into us through praise and thanksgiving.

I would maintain that thanks are the highest form of thought, and that gratitude is happiness doubled by wonder.

— G. K. Chesterton

It had been cool but pleasant that April morning as 29-year-old Agnes Davidson sat on the dock surrounded by luggage. With her three brothers, she was embarking on the greatest adventure of her life—emigration from Ireland to Canada. The transatlantic voyage would sail soon from Southampton in England.

Her brothers had left her to watch the suitcases while they went to celebrate with friends. Now the boat was loading. Passengers from many nationalities and all walks of life were lining up to board ship.

At first, irritation, then apprehension began to grow as the line became shorter. She found herself nearly alone. Where were her brothers? She was desperately torn. She could not leave the bags and sail alone. How could she bear to watch the ship sail without them? Whatever should she do? She dare not leave the luggage to find them. Angry and disappointed, there was absolutely nothing she could do—but watch the huge liner pull away from the pier at 12:00 noon.

The brothers finally arrived, puffing and spluttering. The goodbye celebration with friends at the local pub had become somewhat carried away. They now had to wait in the long lineups to renegotiate tickets. They rushed to catch the train bound for Liverpool where they could take the next available voyage.

Agnes was more than a little annoyed with her brothers. Her anger then turned to immense relief and profound gratefulness as the newswires carried the story. Her brothers' folly had made them too late to take the ill-fated voyage of the Titanic.

One day we will recognize God's hand in our darkest disappointments. We should nor fret, nor complain, but let gratefulness fill our hearts. Soon enough, all will be clear. We will know and understand. God's ways are always best.

Incidentally, Agnes Davidson later became my brother-in-law's grandmother.

Jonah, the rebellious prophet, fled from his responsibilities. A terrible storm trapped the boat where he was stowed. Realizing he had jeopardized every life on the boat, he asked the crew to throw him overboard. God watched over him and prepared a great fish to swallow him. In Jonah 2:5 to 9 we read the prayer of Jonah as he cried out to God from the belly of the fish:

"The engulfing waters threatened me, the deep surrounded me; seaweed was wrapped around my head ... But you brought my life up from the pit, O Lord my God. When my life was ebbing away, I remembered you, Lord, and my prayer rose to you, to your holy temple ... But I, with a song of thanksgiving, will sacrifice to you. What I have vowed I will make good. Salvation comes from the Lord" (NIV).

When Jonah repented, he realized the incredible kindness of the Lord. Instead of punishment, God had extended mercy. While still in the whale, great thankfulness filled his heart. The fish vomited Jonah out onto dry ground.

We also merit nothing of God's favor, yet He has freely given His daily blessings to us. How deeply grateful we should be for His unconditional love and faithfulness.

Even if you've been fishing for three hours and haven't gotten anything except poison ivy and sunburn, you're still better off than the worm.

— Author Unknown

I had arrived in Amsterdam on an early morning flight. After a three-hour layover, I was aboard the plane ready to return to Canada. We were informed that there were some technical difficulties and the mechanics would try to fix the problem while we waited. After sitting in the airplane on the runway for another two hours, it was decided that the problem could not be repaired so easily and that we should wait in the airport terminal.

Four or five hours later, we were given lunch coupons and told to wait a little longer. About nine o'clock in the evening, I, along with approximately 350 other passengers, was informed that we should stay in a complimentary hotel and make the attempt to fly again the next morning.

Every one of these arrangements demanded a line-up: to go through security, to board the airplane, to get off the airplane, to pass through customs, to receive meal vouchers, to receive hotel vouchers, to board the bus to the hotel, and, finally, to check into the hotel. Everyone was exhausted and some tempers were short-fused.

One lady standing somewhere behind me in the line made her protests loud and long. She prattled incessantly about how much trouble these delays were causing her, how her feet hurt, and how she would sue the airline, the airport, and pilot— anyone upon whom she could get her hands. Her grumbling and rumbling echoed up and down the lines where most passengers were standing in stoic silence. Her obnoxious attitude and self-centered monologue jaded frayed nerves.

In the middle of the fatigue and surrounding complaint, I was suddenly overwhelmed with great gratitude. I decided I would rather be on the ground, staying in the complimentary luxury hotel, than be in an airplane experiencing engine failure at 10,000 meters. When we consider the alternatives, our complaints fall into proper perspective. God knows our situation and has everything under control. We are probably much better off than we think!

It is interesting to see how many passages in the Bible refer to gratefulness. Throughout the Old Testament, God commanded that the sacrifices were to be brought before the Lord with thanksgiving. In fact, some offerings were given for the single purpose of expressing gratefulness to God.

Gratitude is an important principle taught all through the Word of God. Even modern science has proven that a thankful heart is a key component to a happy and healthy person. Apostle Paul also emphasized gratefulness in Colossians 2:7:

"Rooted and built up in him, and established in the faith, as ye have been taught, abounding therein with thanksgiving."

A bit of fragrance always clings to the hand that gives you roses.

— Chinese proverb

Scarcely had the winter's ice melted before all nature came alive with the music of birdsong and the brilliance of fresh spring flowers. After weeks of bitter cold and endless fields of snow, the warm sunshine quickly cheered the spirit.

I watched as the birds began to build their nests—every species with a different style of house. Some were meticulously constructed with elaborate architecture; others were barely more than a few sticks thrown together. Although their days were filled with building and searching for food, they took time to stop and sing.

In Matthew chapter 6, Jesus spoke of living with a contented heart. He told how God provided food for the birds and beautiful garments for the flowers in the fields. He warned against anxiety in searching for material possessions and earthly positions. We also need to learn to stop and sing—to be filled with gratefulness for His faithful provision and purposes for our lives.

In the first chapter of Romans, we are shown the ladder by which humanity descended into great moral decay. We read in verses 21 to 24:

"Because that, when they knew God, they glorified him not as God, neither were thankful; but became vain in their imaginations, and their foolish heart was darkened. Professing themselves to be wise, they became fools, And changed the glory of the incorruptible God into an image made like to corruptible man, and to birds, and four-footed beasts, and creeping things. Wherefore God also gave them up...."

Ingratitude is one of the primary attitudes that results in the depravity of mankind. How serious are the consequences of unthankfullness! May we take the challenge to fill our hearts and mouths with thanksgiving.

Do not spoil what you have by desiring what you have not;
but remember that what you now have was once among the things you only hoped for.
— Epicurus

While ministering in a developing country, I made a hasty comment to a co-worker about certain inconveniences that made life less than comfortable in the apartment where we were staying. A young man who was living there overheard my remark. He exclaimed with deep sincerity how genuinely grateful he was for the home, even with all of its imperfections. He invited us to go with him as he emptied the trash basket.

At the back of the large apartment complex was a community dumpster. As we approached, he told us to observe carefully the four or five men and women standing and sitting beside the dumpster. We also noticed the heap of blankets under one of the trees and the eating bowls piled beside them.

The hungry eyes of the strangers followed closely as the fresh garbage was thrown up onto the pile accumulating in the container. Scarcely were our backs turned before the trash we had left had been inspected, sorted, and chosen for survival.

As we retreated to the apartment, I was humbled. Those people by the dumpster had no home. They lived year round under trees or bridges, surviving on pickings from the garbage heaps. Even though I had known that there was much poverty in this city, the extensive material needs of these people affected me profoundly.

I realized, however, a greater poverty was mine. I, who have known so much of western materialism and comforts, found myself poor in thankfulness. Barrenness of gratitude produces roots of bitterness, envy, and discontent. Eventually, it prevents a heart from appreciating all the benefits that one does have. By contrast, happiness and contentment spring spontaneously from the attitude of gratitude.

Lying on my mattress on the floor that night, I repented for my unthankful and complaining attitude. I was safe, warm, dry, and well fed. I had everything I needed for the moment. I knew the Lord was with me. With Him, I had more than enough!

In 1 Samuel 30 we read that the wives and possessions of David and his men had been stolen by a marauding band of Amalekites. Everyone's deep distress because of their loss was tinged with fear for their families. In the confusion and despair of the crisis, they accused David of getting them into the situation. Their frustration fuelled mutinous discussions that began to endanger David's life.

Rather than succumb to hopelessness, David turned his heart to God and His promises. He "...*encouraged himself in the Lord his God*" (1 Samuel 30:6).

As he remembered the faithfulness of God that carried him through past impossibilities, he could find hope for victory in his present challenge. He could think clearly and formulated a plan of attack that resulted in regaining all that had been stolen.

When our hearts are overwhelmed with distress, we also can find peace and courage by changing our focus from the circumstance to the unchanging power of God. Remembering His faithfulness brings gratefulness and assurance. He is our source of wisdom. As we tune our hearts to His voice, He will show us which action plan to take.

There is a world of difference between a person who has a big problem and a person who makes a problem big... the only problem you have is the one you allow to be a problem because of your wrong reaction to it.

— John C. Maxwell

It was one of those days when a number of circumstances had not gone my way. Being an independent soul, I rather enjoy events going according to plan!

Several business telephone calls I needed to make had been thwarted by answering machines telling me that I would be on hold. The one person I did speak to had no idea what I wanted; everyone who knew the pertinent information was going to be on holidays for some weeks.

Frustrated with that endeavor, I tried my hand at baking, which is not my forte, even on good days. The cookies that were produced resembled hockey pucks—black and just as firm!

Taking a break, I decided to wash the kitchen floor—which I succeeded in doing with a flourish by promptly stepping in the bucket. But I discovered improved efficiency because now the water was already all over the floor. I just had to mop it up!

I was frustrated and irritated. I was ripe for an old-fashioned pity-party. My party was put on hold by the phone call of a friend. Tragedy had struck. A loved one had taken ill and the prognosis was uncertain.

As I surveyed the blackened baking and the still-wet floor, I realized that I needed to change my attitude. I had so much to be thankful for. The floor would dry. The cookies could feed some birds (maybe). Eventually, I would get through to the company I needed to speak to on the telephone. But my problems were insignificant in comparison to the heartbreak my friend was experiencing.

As I paused to pray for my friend, I also repented for my self-centered attitude. The frustration and irritation evaporated as I reached out to the Lord for His strength. New courage flooded my heart as gratefulness took the place of complaint, and the assurance of God's intervention brought peace.

It is not possible for a truly grateful heart to retain bitterness or complaint. In the genuine contemplation of our daily benefits, we are humbled to the place of recognizing God's unmerited favor—His grace upon us.

In the receiving of His mercy, there is no place for the pride of bitterness or the arrogance of complaint. The overflowing awareness of the Lord's goodness freely outpoured on us produces springs of deep gratitude.

A thankful heart is not only the greatest virtue, but the parent of all the other virtues.

— Marcus Tullius Cicero

In 1897, a Methodist preacher and prolific songwriter by the name of Johnson Oatman penned the words of the well-known hymn, *Count Your Blessings*. It is impossible to sing or speak this song without recognizing how much we have for which to be thankful. An attitude of gratitude can be released from our hearts.

When upon life's billows you are tempest tossed,
When you are discouraged, thinking all is lost,
Count your many blessings, name them one by one,
And it will surprise you what the Lord hath done.

Refrain
Count your blessings, name them one by one,
Count your blessings, see what God hath done!
Count your blessings, name them one by one,
And it will surprise you what the Lord hath done.

Are you ever burdened with a load of care?
Does the cross seem heavy you are called to bear?
Count your many blessings, every doubt will fly,
And you will keep singing as the days go by.

When you look at others with their lands and gold,
Think that Christ has promised you His wealth untold;
Count your many blessings, money cannot buy
Your reward in heaven, nor your home on high.

So, amid the conflict whether great or small,
Do not be discouraged, God is over all;
Count your many blessings, angels will attend,
Help and comfort give you to your journey's end.

Chapter Three

VITAL VISION

We go toward the direction that we look. It is one of the basic lessons to be aware of when driving a car. If we try to direct our way with our eyes on the scenery, we can soon enough find ourselves part of it.

It is important to focus on that which we aspire to become. For believers, the challenge is to keep our hearts fixed on the Lord. He is our reason for being, the source of salvation, and the goal of eternity. In the light of His glory, everything else grows dim.

When Peter was walking on the water toward Jesus, he was able to live a miracle and experience the impossible—as long as his eyes were fixed on the Lord. As soon as he was distracted by the storm and waves, he lost that capacity.

In Hebrews 12:2, we are admonished to look unto Jesus, the author and finisher of our faith. These words provide one of the most effective keys to a victorious life in Christ. If we look at our circumstances, or the people around us, or concentrate on our own failures, we will lose heart. However, when we keep our lives centered on Christ, we find limitless resources.

The most pathetic person in the world is someone who has sight, but has no vision.

— Helen Keller

The road was completely covered by a five-centimeter layer of ice from one side to the other that stretched for kilometers. Two days' worth of rain and snow had packed it into a slick surface. I drove along slowly in my van, creeping gingerly kilometer after kilometer, white-knuckled tense.

A big black, four-wheel-drive SUV breezed past, full of smiling faces. I stared straight ahead, gently slowing even more as I glumly watched the fancy set of wheels speed on ahead of me. Then, to my amazement, I watched the SUV, now 100 meters distant, jerk this way and that, turn a circle and back deeply into the ditch. It was half buried under the snow! I steadily moved ahead, gingerly passing the vehicle, now full of snow-colored faces and bulging eyeballs! They may have been faster, but I was still crawling forward.

Sometimes we may feel outclassed, out-run, out-everything. Others seem to make bounding progress and prosper at every turn. We may feel left in the dust of those speedier and grander than we.

Be faithful, hold steady, and keep your heart focused on Jesus. The end is not yet! The Lord shall bring us safely through.

In the book of Nehemiah, the enemies of Israel did everything they could to discourage the re-building of the temple and the re-construction of the walls around Jerusalem. In one instance, they asked Nehemiah to come to an unprotected location to meet with them. When he saw their deceitfulness and refused to listen to them, they tried to fill him with fear by suggesting that he stay hidden within a secret closet in the city. Nehemiah refused to be intimidated or sidetracked. He just kept working on the walls.

Often, Satan uses circumstances, people, or evil influences to weaken our perseverance, distract us from our purpose, or hinder our progress. If we consistently keep focused on God's Word, His plan will be fulfilled in us.

Vision is the art of seeing things invisible.

— Jonathan Swift

As I walked down the narrow path through the woods, I admired the majestic trees and listened intently to the songs of various birds. Suddenly, my foot caught on a small root protruding out of the ground. Momentarily, I did some fancy footwork, but to no avail. I was caught off balance and the next thing I knew I was face first in the dirt.

I bounced up lickety-split, glancing around, hoping that no one had witnessed me biting the dust. I quickly brushed myself off and continued on my way more prudently, but none the worse for wear.

Interestingly, it wasn't the large trees that made me fall. I could walk around them. It wasn't the huge rock or the log that lay in the way. It was that pesky little root, scarcely seen, overlooked, seemingly insignificant, that was able to capture me and throw me down.

We must be warned and beware of the snares that Satan has hidden along our way. It is not the huge problems of life that most often catch us, but the little frustrations, personality clashes, and seemingly irrelevant irritations that grate on our minds, poison our attitudes, and flatten us in failure.

The writer of Proverbs pleads with his readers to seek after prudence and wisdom. His admonitions remind us to fear the Lord and to keep Him as the center of who we are. In Proverbs 4:23, we are instructed to,

"Keep thy heart with all diligence;
for out of it are the issues of life."

In the last few years, special emphasis has been placed on diet because unhealthy eating habits usually result in failing health. How much more important it is for us to protect our inner selves. We need to carefully select what we permit ourselves to watch and to hear. What we feed our minds will eventually manifest in our words, attitudes, and actions. What is in the well will come up in the bucket!

Apostle Paul gives guidelines for a successful thought life in Philippians 4:8:

"Finally, brethren, whatsoever things are true, whatsoever things are honest, whatsoever things are just, whatsoever things are pure, whatsoever things are lovely, whatsoever things are of good report; if there be any virtue, and if there be any praise, think on these things."

Never go to a doctor whose office plants have died.
— Erma Bombeck

Accommodations were somewhat primitive by western standards in the eastern European country where I was ministering. In the apartment where we were staying, we had been suspicious of unwanted four-legged furry visitors for a couple of days. In fact, I had resorted to stuffing pillows into some cracks that were near where I slept on a mattress on the floor.

As I passed through the kitchen, a sudden movement caught my eye. A rat ran down the water pipe and disappeared behind the stove. With a screech, I fled the room! At the same instant, my friend was reading aloud from a book describing a poor boy who had awakened in a varmint-infested barn to find a rat sleeping on his chest. The coincidence seemed prophetic.

Determined to catch the intruder, we set two traps. For two days, every time we went out, the bait was stolen from both traps. On the third day, the sneaky thief stole the bait, the trap, and all! This was getting serious. The stove was moved and every corner inspected. The thief returned.

Finally, a sort of cement was used to fill every crack and crevice. That solved the problem.

Satan is treacherous, seeking to steal, kill, and destroy. Through the reasoning of our minds and crevices in our character, in unwary moments, he attempts to thwart God's work in us. It is not sufficient to recognize him or trap him on our territory. We must prevent his entry and influence in our lives. We must fill every rat hole, reject every excuse, and keep our hearts with all diligence.

Many believers struggle to keep their priorities focused on eternal values. Under the stress of constant materialistic and humanistic bombardment, many have succumbed to a Christianity of convenience. The effort of church attendance, Bible study, and even prayer has given way to resignation and apathy.

We cannot tell when we actually fall asleep. Once we get comfortable and drowsy, sleep just happens. In the parable of the ten virgins in Matthew 25, Jesus speaks of this exact scenario. May the Lord help us shake ourselves and be renewed in passion for Christ, lest we also be caught unaware and unprepared at His return.

Dissatisfaction and discouragement are not caused by the absence of things but the absence of vision.

— Author Unknown

I had been invited to share a bountiful meal with friends. Later, sitting in the sunshine on the balcony, I began to feel extremely drowsy. Even the cup of potent coffee had not succeeded in chasing away the intense desire for a nap. With all my strength, I tried to concentrate on the conversation. At times, the lady's face opposite me seemed to blur into a dream about a soft couch. I wrestled with the desire to stretch out on the bench, the floor—anything flat.

"Just five minutes," I argued, "that is all I need."

Dignity, or pride—I'm not sure which—kept me sitting bolt upright, blinking my glassy eyes in the direction of the last voice that spoke. At last it was time to move on. The act of simply standing up seemed to lift the fuzz out of my head.

On the more serious note, it seems that many Christians have settled into a similar place of comfort. They are not really sleeping, but they surely would like to be. Well-fed, nurtured, and loved, many have become numbed by the inactivity of being spectators instead of active participants in the Christian faith. Apostle Paul challenged the believers in Romans 13:11 and 12:

"And that, knowing the time, that now it is high time to awake out of sleep: for now is our salvation nearer than when we believed. The night is far spent, the day is at hand: let us therefore cast off the works of darkness, and let us put on the armour of light."

The schedule had been unusually heavy for several weeks. After entering the quietness of the guestroom where I was staying, I sank into a chair, overcome with a sense of profound weariness. The fatigue quickly produced the following questions: Why am I doing this? To what avail are my efforts? What is the point of struggling on?

Emotional and physical fatigue breeds discouragement in our minds. In Galatians 6:9, Apostle Paul encourages us to keep our focus during times when we become disheartened:

"Let us not become weary in doing good, for at the proper time we will reap a harvest if we do not give up" (NIV).

Rest and relaxation are normal and healthy, but only to gain renewed passion for Christ and His Kingdom. We must not succumb to lethargy and laziness. Let vision be renewed in our hearts as we come alive to His highest purposes.

A bend in the road is not the end of the road... unless you fail to make the turn.
— Author Unknown

The road seemingly stretched out to infinity. The sun was shining. The yellow line was hypnotic. I was so comfortable. The car was getting warmer and warmer as I got sleepier and sleepier. My mind was slowly numbing to impending disaster. *Disaster*! The thought suddenly snapped me back to reality! Calamity was impending, but I was becoming too comfortable to realize it. The time for radical action had come. Stop and walk around the car! Turn on the radio! Pull off and take a nap! *Do* something!

We become aware that we are tired or drowsy. We know we are relaxed but we can't actually tell the moment we fall asleep. Unfortunately, the same is true in our spiritual life. We become comfortable, as soul-numbing apathy creeps over us. Unaware, we drift into spiritual unconsciousness. When slumber is deep, we may need a blaring alarm to awaken us.

Jesus commanded us in Matthew 26:41:

"Watch and pray, that ye enter not into temptation...."

We need the Lord's help to recognize our peril, shake ourselves to action, and be awakened from our apathy before the strike of spiritual catastrophe.

In Colossians 3:2, we are admonished: "*Set your affection on things above, not on things on the earth.*"

Our hearts can easily be captivated with the pressures of seeking and caring for material possessions. We are pressured by marketing to purchase more than we can afford, for assets we don't need. Our minds are continuously bombarded with enticements encouraging discontentment with what we have.

Distressing circumstances and setbacks, the anxiety of rising prices and future uncertainties can also fill our thoughts. On every hand, distractions try to deter us from eternal values. But the Word of God tells us that the secret to peace in these troubled times is to rivet our passions on things above.

*Don't tell me what your priorities are.
Show me where you spend your money
and I'll tell you what they are.*
— James W. Frick

The precious daughter of dear friends was going to be married within a week. The excitement of preparation was palpable. The families were large and the guest list was filled to capacity. Suddenly, news of serious illness meant that several guests would be unable to attend. The meal had already been paid for; the places would be empty. In that last moment an invitation was extended to me. I was thrilled with the honor and delighted to participate in the wedding and celebrations, literally, in someone else's place.

The experience reminded me of the story Jesus relates in Luke 14:16 to 24. Jesus replied:

> *A certain man was preparing a great banquet and invited many guests. At the time of the banquet he sent his servant to tell those who had been invited, "Come, for everything is now ready." But they all alike began to make excuses. The first said, "I have just bought a field and I must go and see it. Please excuse me." Another said, "I have just bought five yoke of oxen, and I'm on my way to try them out. Please excuse me." Still another said, "I just got married, so I can't come."*
>
> *The servant came back and reported this to his master. Then the owner of the house became angry and ordered his servant, "Go out quickly into the streets and alleys of the town and bring in the poor, the crippled, the blind, and the lame." "Sir," the servant said, "what you ordered has been done, but there is still room." Then the master told his servant, "Go out to the roads and country lanes and make them come in, so that my house will be full. I tell you, not one of those men who were invited will get a taste of my banquet." (NIV).*

God has made preparations for us to celebrate with Him. Each day, He has a rich banquet prepared for us, if only we would take the time to wait in His presence. Often we make excuses because our activities seem of greater importance. The Lord is calling all who will to come, even telling His servants to compel people to come. Let us quickly respond with joy to the tremendous honor that has been extended to us.

Chapter Four

PATIENT PERSEVERANCE

Someone has said that success in almost any field takes about ten percent ability but about ninety percent tenacity. Potential may be immense, but unless there is perseverance, it will probably never be fully realized. Often, we have seen highly talented people who never fulfilled expectations because they lacked determination to carry through with their dreams.

The joy of accomplishment brings profound satisfaction—but it can only be experienced after the work is completed. A friend told me that when she was a little girl someone asked her what she wanted to be when she grew up, to which she replied, "I would like to be a returned missionary." Having heard the exciting adventures (and misadventures) of missionaries, she concluded that she would love to be able to tell such stories without having to go through the difficult experiences.

There are no shortcuts in reaching worthy goals. By building on the wisdom gleaned from past experience, we have an established foundation for future opportunities.

In Philippians 3:13 and 14, Apostle Paul gives this challenge:

"...forgetting those things which are behind, and reaching forth unto those things which are before, I press toward the mark for the prize of the high calling of God in Christ Jesus."

On the frontier of each new day let us lay aside every hindrance. With purpose, we pursue the presence of God.

Some individuals live continually burdened with the regrets of yesterday. This painful and profitless exercise robs them of the strength to live in the present. Others are looking ahead with such anticipation they neglect the enjoyment of this moment.

A teacher friend related the following illustration. Ten-year-old twin girls were on a two-day school field trip. As they went from one historical site to the next, the girls kept asking, "When are we leaving here? Where are we going next?" When the trip was over, they had not appreciated the moment-by-moment experiences because of their continual expectation of a greater thrill. There is a balance in which we build upon our past experience, filled with hope for the future, while loving and living life to its maximum today.

The only place the past can live is in your memory.
The only power it has over you is the power you give it.
— Author Unknown

People have been known to be exceptionally fond of their pets. In fact, they can be treated with more tender loving care than children. Some people become so attached to their animals they find it impossible to part with them. I noticed this at one place where I stayed.

Unique dust covers were thrown over the ends of several couches in the living room. They looked like cat skins! I commented to the hostess about the furry covers. She replied that she dearly loved her cats and when they died she had them skinned. She could be reminded of them every time she looked at the dusters on her furniture.

A time comes when it is necessary to let some things go. Sentimental attachments are precious; memories of past blessings can generate gratitude. Beautiful experiences can remind us of God's faithfulness. But if the cat dies—bury it—bury it all!

Some individuals dwell in the past, continually regurgitating the wonderful days of yesteryear. Doubtless they were great, but let us find blessings for today.

A pastor friend of mine was energetically leading the singing during the Sunday service. The song was lively and, with exuberance he sang with all his might when, to his astonishment—and the amusement of the congregation—his dentures flew out of his mouth. To the delight of the audience, he caught them in midair, popped them back in, and never missed a beat. From that moment, he had the full attention of the crowd. In fact, it was a worship service to remember because everyone forgot petty distractions and entered without reservation into worshiping the Lord.

Rapid response in a crisis can certainly save the day—and may even save face! There are opportunities that come only once in a lifetime. We need to be alert and ready at every instant. Though circumstances may be crushing or humiliating, don't park in them. Seize the moment, change your attitude, and discover unknown dimensions of courage and blessings.

Be brave! Even if you're not, pretend to be.
No one can tell the difference.

— Author Unknown

A large cardboard box that I wanted to use had some dust in the bottom so I stepped outside in order to shake it out. With the box held high, I flipped it over while taking a stride to one side. Before realizing what was even happening, I did a nose dive down two steps onto the cement sidewalk, landing with my head in the box!

It took a moment to shake myself free. Slowly, I tested each arm and leg to make sure all appendages were still functioning. Apart from minor scrapes and an insulted sense of pride, I suffered no serious consequences. I hastily got on my feet to continue my tasks.

It had happened so fast and without warning. Unfortunately, not all of life's tumbles end as well. There are financial setbacks, family conflicts, failures, sickness, and tragedies that arrive unexpectedly and can leave terrible scars. Some losses may never be recovered.

Whatever has happened in our lives, it is important for us to stand up within ourselves, make some attitude adjustments, and walk on through the possibilities the Lord sets before us. An old adage reminds us, "It is not the one who falls who fails, but the one who refuses to rise up again."

Every four years the news is filled with the successes or failures of Olympic contestants, who have trained for years to compete in specific events. Each athlete's purpose, focus, and single-minded dedication is to excel in the chosen sport, win a gold medal, and receive the applause of the world—a fleeting moment of glory.

In Hebrews 12:1, we are reminded that we also are in a race with far greater consequences and rewards:

"…let us lay aside every weight, and the sin which doth so easily beset us, and let us run with patience the race that is set before us."

The following verse admonishes us to also have a single-minded focus:

"Looking unto Jesus the author and finisher of our faith…."

That is the key. Not only is *He* our goal, He supplies the courage and strength to achieve His highest purposes as we run the race.

Endurance is not just the ability to bear a hard thing, but to turn it into glory.

— William Barclay

The country lanes of England are picturesque. The gentle rolling pastures are crisscrossed by stone fences and dotted with grazing sheep. After arriving in the northern county of Durham, and sensing the need for some air and exercise, I set out for a walk. If I followed the directions of my hostess and kept turning left on the narrow roads I would be able to make a three-kilometer circle.

The last turn was due any minute. Still I walked. I asked a passerby and she indicated that the turn was just ahead. I continued to walk. Had I missed it? The sun began to set. Where was that last little path? I could see the farm less than half a kilometer away, but the road to it completely eluded me. Becoming anxious, I made the decision to abandon the search and walk back the way I had come.

With tender, tired feet and much later than planned, I finally arrived where I had started. I quizzed my friend on the whereabouts of the elusive path. I was informed that if I had continued to walk less than 100 meters, I would have found it, and saved myself the three-kilometer return walk.

We may be tempted to abandon goals and higher purposes—even when they are in sight. The way seems long. Uncertain, we choose to take the road better known and rest in the security of comfortable paths. In Luke 18:1, we read this challenge:

"Then Jesus told his disciples...that they should always pray and not give up" (NIV).

We must not give up. One more step, one more curve may yield the longed-for answer. Keep walking on.

Daily frustrations can wear us out. We are left exhausted—spiritually, physically, and emotionally. Romans 8:37 dares to declare however:

"...in all these things we are more than conquerors through him that loved us."

Even present circumstances cannot separate us from the love of God. In the problem, in the crisis, in the conflict, He is there with us.

We may not understand the causes or have the solutions at present, but His unfailing love will give us courage and faith in every situation. When every other source of hope has fled, the love of God will hold us fast.

The Lord has promised sufficient grace for every experience of life. In all things, at all times, we will have all we need to accomplish His will. Let us lift up our hearts with hope. He will forgive us, sustain us, and empower us for His purposes.

By perseverance the snail reached the ark.
— Charles Haddon Spurgeon

The struggle was intense, with only brief lapses of rest. At times it seemed too difficult, but slowly, surely, victory came. At last the butterfly emerged from the cocoon. He stretched his multicolored wings, wiggled his antennae, and rested, shimmering in the sunlight for several minutes as though amazed at his transformation from an ugly grub. Then, on a puff of wind he was off, fluttering gleefully over the flowers, daintily tasting here and there.

Science has discovered that the struggle of getting out of the confining cocoon is necessary to develop sufficient strength for the butterfly to fly once it is free. Without this wrestling against resistance, it would not be able to survive.

The desperate conflicts we face are also necessary to develop strength of soul. We may cry out for easier ways or quick escapes from our crises. The pressures may seem impossible and intense. However, the character and courage for future flight will only be achieved through present struggles. Don't give up. We shall soon fly free on wings of grace.

Newspapers are filled with horrific news of natural disasters, global warming, and nuclear bombs. There is death by war, famine, and disease. Although the Word of God clearly depicts these and other dreadful events yet to happen, the Bible brings everything into proper perspective in God's ultimate scheme of things—the imminent return of Jesus.

Rather than being paralyzed by fear, we lift up our hearts with hope. That is what Jesus Himself told us to do in Luke 21:28:

"And when these things begin to come to pass, then look up, and lift up your heads; for your redemption draweth nigh."

Through the promises of God's Word we are challenged to continue. Rather than being disheartened by crises, we have anticipation and expectation of divine intervention.

What counts is not necessarily the size of the dog in the fight— it's the size of the fight in the dog.
— Dwight D. Eisenhower

As soon as I entered my garden shed I knew something was wrong. My wheelbarrow had been tipped over. Two tin cans were turned over in the middle of the floor. There had been an intruder!

After further investigation, I discovered that some fibreglass insulation had been turned into a large ball on a shelf. Who would do such a thing? Then, when I looked into some tin cans where nails were kept, I discovered they were packed to the brim with spruce cones. A twenty-liter garden pail had been over half-filled with cones. Thousands of cones filled every corner of the building. Then I knew the identity of my visitor—a squirrel!

Patiently preparing for winter, he had turned every corner of my shed into his lunch larder, filling it with his food stashes. The insulation had been turned into cosy sleeping quarters for him and his family. Unfortunately, he had also chewed a hole in a corner of the wall for fast getaways. I was not impressed!

With no sympathy whatsoever, I bundled his handiwork into the garbage and swept the place clean of his bits and pieces. I firmly nailed shut his self-made doorway.

After my fury was pacified, I had to admit, valuable lessons were to be learned from the furry little fellow:

* Preparation: While the winter winds blew, he was planning to be warm and well fed.
* Perseverance: Day after day he was foraging for food, making thousands of trips to stow it away.
* Patience: One by one he was adding to the myriads of cones to store enough for the family.
* Productivity: He was making purposeful use of his life and time.
* Pluck: He had the nerve to face the neighbourhood's hungry cats, barking dogs, and pellet guns to carry on his duties.

All of these are valuable life lessons. I began to feel slightly sorry that I had thrown out all the hard-earned food stores of the little creature—but not sorry enough to invite him back.

The piles of packed, hardened snow around the house were at least a meter deep. As the warm spring sun beat on them, one could almost see them shrinking. Within a few days they had disappeared completely, turning into puddles and rivulets everywhere.

Sometimes the obstacles confronting us seem impossible and impassable. However, the light of God's presence, the warmth of His love, and the power of His Spirit can melt the hardest heart and transform mountains into rivers of joy.

Always listen to the experts.
They'll tell you what can't be done and why.
Then do it.

— Robert Heinlein

The traffic was backed up for several kilometers. It didn't matter which lane we were in, it was the one that was not moving. I guess they call that Murphy's Law.

After creeping forward for nearly an hour, my friend and I observed a truck passing in the lane beside us. It was carrying three large trees standing nearly upright. I dryly remarked to my friend that now I knew we were not making much progress. Even the trees were passing us!

Sometimes in our relationship with the Lord we may feel that we are at a complete standstill. It may seem as though God is moving in every situation except in the one where we are stuck. Imperceptibly but steadily, He will bring us through. Persevere. Step by step we will advance as we keep our focus on Christ.

Chapter Five

HELD BY HOPE

A pilot friend told me the importance of the instrument panel when flying an aircraft. The real test, however, is to *trust* that the instruments are telling the truth.

While piloting an aircraft in whiteout conditions, for example, he told me every sense may signal the plane is descending, even though the altimeter reads that all is well. The natural instinct is to abandon the training and fly by feelings. However, one must trust the dials and continue to fly. How comforting to see the lights of the airport and know one had been guided safely by trusting the instrument panel. He affirmed that following this rule had spared his life on more than one occasion.

We have the promises of God's Word and the quiet inner voice of His Holy Spirit softly directing and holding us through the darkest hours of our lives. In spite of overwhelming circumstances, sorrow, or uncertain future, let us affirm our confidence in Christ and hold fast to the hope we have in Him. The night will pass and joy will come in the morning.

Two men, blinded by disappointment and disillusionment, walked slowly down the road to Emmaus. They had seen Jesus die. In their discussions they tried to make sense of what they had witnessed—the amazing life and then this horrifying death of the One they had believed was the Messiah.

The stranger who joined them seemed to know nothing of these catastrophic events. Why, all of Jerusalem was abuzz with the news!

"Where have you been?" they exclaimed. "How is it that you know nothing of these happenings?"

As they poured out their dismay and confusion, He listened patiently. With firm, but gentle reproof, He showed them from the scriptures who He was. In one brilliant revelation they saw Him—they knew Him. He had been there all the time! He knew more about these events than they did!

How often we walk the lonely road of discouragement, sure that we are alone, forgotten, and abandoned. Look up! Jesus knows more about our situation than we do! Veiled, perhaps, behind our momentary distress—but He is there. We have His promise in Matthew 28:20:

"...I am with you always, even unto the end of the world. Amen."

He walks the road with us.

God's promises are like the stars;
the darker the night
the brighter they shine.

— David Nicholas

The kilometers ticked by as I steadily drove toward my destination. I became more and more anxious as I thought of the possible conflict that awaited me. A difficult situation from a previous visit to this location made me apprehensive.

By the time I arrived, my heart was pounding, I had a slight headache, my hands were wet with perspiration, and I was in full-flight mode. What if...? Everything was prefixed by this tormenting phrase. Anxiety, even panic, had filled my mind. My mind was screaming, "Turn around! Go home!"

But when I arrived I was warmly welcomed. Genuine sweetness filled the atmosphere. My anxieties evaporated. The visit became a memory filled with love and goodwill.

All those kilometers of worry were for nothing! The pounding heart, the perspiration, the imaginary conversations full of fright and defense were a total waste of time.

How many wasted hours of life have been filled with frightful but needless imaginations and anxieties? Jesus told us not to worry about the clothes we wear or the food we eat. May the Lord help us to practise trust in Him instead of worrying.

Hezekiah was deeply troubled because the enemy—the brutal, unstoppable Assyrian empire—planned to destroy him and the entire nation of Judah. He took their threatening letter into the temple of God and spread it out before the Lord. He called upon God for a solution. The Lord heard and sent the prophet Isaiah with words of hope and victory. In short order, the enemy was defeated and God's people were spared.

We can likewise lay our burdens before the Lord. We can open His Word and remind God of His promises. In His time and His way, He will reveal His power on our behalf as we walk on with Him.

It is easy to turn a molehill into a mountain. You just have to add a little dirt.

— Author Unknown

Having been raised on a farm, I am not terribly terrified by mice, although I certainly do not enjoy their company. By contrast, my co-worker demonstrated her fright by performing an exotic jig on the bed when a mouse was seen in the apartment where we were staying. We baited some traps and hoped to catch it. After the service, we found the traps had done their duty and caught two mice. We reset the traps and went to sleep.

Suddenly, at 1:43 a.m. I was jolted out of a dead sleep when, with a screech, my dear friend and fellow laborer jumped onto my bed! Trembling like a leaf, she informed me that a mouse had been caught in the trap in her room. Not yet dead, it was flapping the trap around with every frantic jump. With the skill of a trapeze artist, she had used the chairs as stilts to flee from the room.

Now she perched on her tiptoes on my bed, pleading with me to put the creature out of its misery and to please protect her from the dire consequences of a mouse running up her leg. By the time I collected my wits—plus my shoes, flashlight, and a sturdy broom—the poor fellow was dead.

In the darkness of our midnights, our imaginations can make little mice seem as powerful and dangerous as roaring lions. Insignificant problems can take on enormous proportions, paralyzing us with fear and dread. The reality of our danger is far less than our perception. It is important to keep our perspective aligned with God's Word.

While reading the Psalms, I have often been struck by how relevant they are in modern life and circumstance. On one occasion recently, when I reflected on some of my personal inadequacies and failures, guilt and gloom began to settle over my mind like a cold, wet blanket. Opening the Word of God for direction and consolation, Psalm 130:1 to 5 leaped off the page and met the need of my heart:

Out of the depths I cry to you, O Lord;
O Lord, hear my voice.
Let your ears be attentive
to my cry for mercy.
If you, O Lord, kept a record of sins,
O Lord, who could stand?
But with you there is forgiveness;
therefore you are feared.
I wait for the Lord, my soul waits,
and in his word I put my hope (NIV).

The promises of God's Word are relevant and powerful for us in every situation today. Let us stand firm in faith. God is with us.

The pessimist sees difficulty in every opportunity.
The optimist sees the opportunity in every difficulty.
— Winston Churchill

When I told the pastor I would like to go to the post office, he readily agreed to drive me there. He informed me, however, that parking nearby would be nearly impossible. He offered to drop me off at the door of the post office and drive his little white car around the block until I had completed my business. When I came out of the building, I could watch for him and get into the car again as he passed by.

Having finished my business, I came out of the post office. I saw the little white car right there waiting at the red light. Quick as a flash I pulled open the door and jumped inside before the light would change. The young man who was driving the car looked at me with eyes like dinner plates. This fellow was *not the pastor*! He quickly grabbed his briefcase while staring at me wide-eyed.

"Ooops, wrong car!" I exclaimed—and with enormous speed, sailed out of the car. The light changed and the young man sped away. Then I spotted the pastor's vehicle approaching. Blushing feverishly, I crawled in, hoping he had not seen my mistake. He had, and was in a fit of laughter. To this day he has never let me forget it.

Sometimes we jump into situations too quickly. We can easily find ourselves in distressing crises because of our haste or miscalculations. It is indeed our assurance—and often only hope—that the Lord will guide us through each circumstance.

In Hebrews 11:8, the Bible reads:

"By faith Abraham, when he was called to go out into a place which he was to receive as an inheritance, obeyed; and he went out, not knowing whither he went."

For Abraham, the future was an unknown road. But he had received God's promise and that was sufficient for total obedience and trust.

We have moments when we wish we could know what the future holds. The uncertainty can cause us to be troubled and distressed. However, God has given us His promises and His presence, His peace and His power—Himself. As we walk in obedience like Abraham, we know our tomorrows are in His hands. That is all the future we need to know.

I believe in the sun, even when it is not shining.
I believe in love, even when I feel it not.
I believe in God, even when He is silent.

— Written on a wall in a concentration camp

A friend of mine has an uncanny ability to get lost while driving. On one occasion, she spent a whole day driving in the fog hoping to arrive at her destination several hundred kilometers distant, only to discover after seven hours of driving that she had done a number of circles and was in fact still very near home. Needless to say, that adventure has earned her a reputation, which she has succeeded in keeping through several similar episodes since.

When another friend heard of her dilemma, he offered her a gift of a Global Positioning System (GPS) gadget. She can now enter the address of her destination, drive hundreds of kilometers, and arrive just in front of the door. That device even has an automated voice telling her when to turn. With its direct connection to satellites, she never needs to be lost again—even in the densest fog.

We can also have clear directions for the journey of life. The Lord, who can see the beginning and the end, can clearly show us the way, even in the darkest night. As we set our destination for heaven and home, Psalm 32:8 reminds us that God will hold our hand and guide our way:

"I will instruct thee and teach thee in the way which thou shalt go: I will counsel thee with mine eye upon thee" (ASV).

When we are faced with various circumstances or sense the concern for world events, we may find it difficult to know how to pray. In these times, I am so thankful for the promise and principle of Romans 8:26 and 27:

"Likewise the Spirit also helps in our weaknesses. For we do not know what we should pray for as we ought, but the Spirit Himself makes intercession for us with groanings which cannot be uttered. Now He who searches the hearts knows what the mind of the Spirit is, because He makes intercession for the saints according to the will of God" (NKJV).

We cannot know what the future holds. However, we have the assurance of God's presence to lead the way.

I do not understand it but I just keep trusting my Good Shepherd because I know He will not lead me any place He does not want me to follow.

— Alice Marquardt

Minutes before my friend and I were to be introduced to sing and speak in the service, she urgently leaned over and whispered, "I have a huge hole in the back of my stocking!" We were due to go on the platform immediately. What could she do?

Thinking quickly, I suggested that she walk directly in front of me onto the platform; I would follow closely behind her. In that way we hoped no one would espy the torn hose.

According to plan, after introductions, I followed on her heels—too close, in fact, to notice a guitar case that had been left open beside the stairs. Too late to see the danger, I stumbled into the guitar case and unceremoniously sat in it! Of course no one noticed my friend's stocking! They were far too busy stifling their laughter as I crawled out of the case and up the stairs.

How often we try to avoid potential hazards only to open the door to more sinister calamities. We must trust the unforeseen into the hands of the One who sees and knows.

Modern technology has given us instant communication via telephone, e-mail, voice mail... However, it is not always so instant! It can be very aggravating to work through five minutes of being told, "push 2 for this, push 4 for that, push 3 for something else..." only to be put on hold! What a relief to eventually be able to speak to a real live person.

How incredible and marvellous that we can have truly instant access to the King of Kings! In Hebrews 4:16 we are given the extraordinary invitation:

"Let us then approach the throne of grace with confidence, so that we may receive mercy and find grace to help us in our time of need" (NIV).

Call on God, but row away from the rocks.

— Indian proverb

The auditorium was packed. A number of ladies were clearing the tables as I prepared to address the crowd after a delicious supper. To my right was an aisle between tables where they were carrying food and table wares. As I began to sing, to my utter horror, I saw a large spider slowly dropping down from the ceiling directly over the passageway where the ladies were walking. One large hairdo approached, and with millimeters to spare, safely walked on, blissfully unaware of the threat dangling over her head.

In the middle of my song, I could not warn anyone; neither dare I draw attention to the assailant, lest I cause pandemonium. I could envision the spider catching a ride on someone's head and the panic that could result as everyone sought to find it and murder it. I could do nothing but finish my song, keeping one wary eye on the unwelcome visitor. Much to my relief, his plans changed and he began to ascend his ladder to the lofty heights above.

Innocently we tread past unseen and unknown dangers. But they do not escape the eye of the Lord. Only eternity will reveal the multitude of deliverances God's hand has provided. Let our hearts be filled with trust that He will never leave us nor forsake us.

The book of Lamentations portrays the deep mourning of Jeremiah the prophet. He saw by revelation the calamities that would fall upon Israelis because of their sin. However, in Lamentations 3:22 to 25, he lifted his gaze from the destruction and sorrow to focus on the heart of God. It was then he wrote:

"It is of the Lord's mercies that we are not consumed, because his compassions fail not. They are new every morning: great is thy faithfulness. The Lord is my portion, sayeth my soul; therefore will I hope in him."

What joy! What comfort! The mercy and compassion of God are without measure. In troubled times—when stock markets tumble, when wars rumble, when human kingdoms crumble, and human hearts are terrified—He abides faithful. Our hope is secure in Him.

God is too good to be unkind,
He is too wise to be mistaken,
and when you can't trace His hand,
that's when you must learn to trust His heart.
— Author Unknown

A pastor and his wife, who became my dear friends, ministered in several remote northern communities. He supported himself and his family with a painting business. A number of profitable contracts had permitted him to build his own home. He stored his painting supplies in the basement.

One night, as the family slept a fire broke out and spread rapidly through the structure. Within minutes the oil paint in the basement caught fire and the building exploded into flames. The pastor only had time to awaken his wife and scream for his children. They plunged out into the bitterly cold January night wearing nothing but nightclothes, saving only their lives. Miraculously, all of the family was safe.

Neighbours and firemen quickly converged on the fire. However, the heat was so intense from the burning paint and oily materials there was nothing anyone could do. They watched helplessly as the house was completely destroyed. The family was taken to the home of an elderly woman to lodge for the night.

When morning came, with trembling heart my friend wrapped himself in blankets topped off with the elderly woman's high boots, fur coat, and hat. He ventured over to the smouldering ruins of his home. Standing with the watchful firemen, he gazed down into the rubble that had collapsed into the basement.

At that moment, something unusual happened. He did not expect it and he had no words to describe what came over him. While standing beside the charred timbers, an inexplicable joy and peace flooded his mind. He suddenly began to laugh, bursting out with praise to God.

The pastor cut an outrageous and somewhat ridiculous figure as he stood in the snow, draped in the woman's too-small fur coat, high-heeled boots, and hat—laughing hilariously as the tears coursed through the soot on his face. The attending firemen were sure he had lost his mind.

He explained that at that moment he had been filled with an intense awareness of God's presence. He *knew* that the Lord would bring him through this crisis. Although his home and business were gone, his faith and family were secure. The material loss was nothing in comparison to the assurance that God was in control.

Sure enough, as the days passed, every need was supplied, prosperity returned, and God proved His faithfulness in multiplied blessings. Psalmist David sang it this way in Psalm 42:5:

"Why are you downcast, O my soul? Why so disturbed within me? Put your hope in God, for I will yet praise him..." (NIV).

The Book of Psalms is filled with the praises and prayers of David and others as they wrestle with the challenges of life. Human frustrations and fragilities are expressed to God as hearts cry out for divine answers to daily dilemmas.

After listing grievances and anguishes, the songs surge to the heights of confidence in the faithfulness and mercy of the Lord. After all the complaint, anxiety, and despair, the writers conclude that God's Word is true, His promises sure, His hope eternal, His love unfailing, His character blameless, and His mercy everlasting.

Like the writers of the Psalms, we have moments when we pour out our fretfulness and fears, our frustrations and feebleness before Him. Assured by His unchanging Word, our hearts then lift in songs of praise to Him.

An atheist is a man who has no invisible means of support.
— Bishop Fulton Sheen

In January 1987, my brother-in-law, Cory, contracted the job of building a winter road. It would traverse about 200 kilometers of forest, swamp, and lakes. Shortly after beginning the road construction, Cory and his crew reached the first lake.

Around noon, the men were driving snow removal equipment on the lake, widening the ice-road. The ice had been tested for thickness but no one could see two pressure cracks joining at an angle along the designated route.

Cory was driving a front-end loader, pushing the snow aside when he felt the back wheels drop. He stood up to get out of the machine but before he could escape, the pie shaped piece of ice at the point of the pressure cracks broke off. The machine slid backwards into the lake.

The ice broke the back window of the cab and Cory, a non-swimmer, was able to gasp one deep breath before the cab filled with water. The turbulence and ice pushed the front window out, drawing him out as well. However, he was sucked rapidly downwards by the turbulence, while being tossed and battered by large chunks of ice.

Although he determined to stay conscious as long as possible, he realized that he might not survive. He was filled with the peace of God. He was ready—either way.

The only hope of survival would be to surface through the same three-meter hole broken open by the falling machine. To miss that small opening would be certain death. The chances of coming up again at that exact location in the middle of an ice-covered lake were very slim indeed.

He caught a tiny glimpse of light, like a star on a foggy night. It was the sun reflecting off the broken ice. Suddenly, he popped to the surface in the hole between chunks of ice—a huge miracle!

However, he now needed another divine intervention. No one had seen him and the machine plunge into the lake. The blowing snow soon iced him over as he clung to a floating block of ice. Hypothermia posed a deadly threat.

The snow removal vehicle following after him arrived about ten minutes later. The driver didn't see the hole in the ice and almost drove in on top of Cory. Suddenly—just in time—he could distinguish my nearly submerged brother-in-law shouting at him from the hole.

Other men arrived and he was pulled to safety. After returning to their base camp for dry clothes, he was transported sixteen kilometers on a sled behind a snowmobile to a remote medical clinic. From there he was air lifted to a hospital. The next day, he was released with only minor injuries. Three days later he was back working on the winter road.

Life, at best, is uncertain. How marvellous that we can face life or death with the assurance that, whatever happens, we are the Lord's. For the believer there is *always* hope. God shared His heart with His people in Jeremiah 29:11:

"For I know the plans I have for you," declares the Lord, *"plans to prosper you and not to harm you, plans to give you hope and a future"* (NIV).

Fear is one of the most debilitating forces of the human heart. Apart from the natural self-preservation instinct, much fear is linked to our imagination of what might happen—but probably won't. It is closely associated with worry and anxiety.

Someone has said that more than 98 percent of the catastrophes we worry about will never happen. The small percentage that do happen never take place the way we expect. We can determine not to let unfounded anxieties damage our tomorrows before they have even arrived. Instead, we can rest in the principle and the promise of Philippians 4:6 and 7:

"Do not be anxious about anything, but in everything, by prayer and petition, with thanksgiving, present your requests to God. And the peace of God, which transcends all understanding, will guard your hearts and your minds in Christ Jesus" (NIV).

*Take charge of your attitude.
Don't let someone else choose it for you.
— Author Unknown*

The sidewalk had ended. I continued to walk along the side of the road facing the oncoming traffic. I was somewhat oblivious to the passing cars as I approached the driveway of a local business. A large four-wheel drive half-ton truck was waiting to exit onto the highway. I stepped in front of it as the driver waited for the traffic to clear.

I did not realize he had not seen me because the passing cars had distracted him. Suddenly he started to move. I was directly in front of the truck with nowhere to go, and no time to flee. I shouted loudly and banged my hand on the hood of his truck. He stopped. The truck pressed tightly against me. Another few centimeters and I would have been knocked down beneath it.

When I approached the driver, I could see his pale face and expression of horror. In fact, he looked downright green! He reached out his hand to me and asked if I was all right. I assured him that I was fine. Then I suddenly said, "I could have died, but at least I know where I am going. I would have been with Jesus."

With eyes still filled with fright, he exclaimed, "I'm so thankful I didn't kill you!" I told him that there is a God in heaven that loves him and me—One who is faithful to care for us—and I continued on my journey.

It was some moments later that the full impact of the episode hit me (no pun intended). Indeed, our lives at any moment are one breath—one heartbeat—from eternity. What hope we have in Christ! Our times are in His hands. How comforting to be able to face life or death with equal assurance that God is always in control.

Chapter Six

SUFFICIENT SALVATION

God specializes in producing miracles out of the most unlikely materials. To start with, He used mud to make man and a rib to make woman! Jesus used a boy's lunch to feed a multitude, an adulterous woman to convict the self-righteous, a demon-possessed man to touch a city, and a cross to bring salvation to the world.

From the abundant resources of His omnipotence there is no prayer He cannot hear, no need He cannot supply, no sickness He cannot heal, and no sin He cannot forgive. There is also no limit to His infinite wisdom, which He gives, not according to our wishes, but according to His will.

His is the amazing grace that picks up the fallen and empowers them to stand. In Him we find the source of life, joy, peace, and power—the never-ending supply of Himself.

In 1 Corinthians 1:26 to 29, Paul reminds us:

"...think of what you were when you were called. Not many of you were wise by human standards; not many were influential; not many were of noble birth. But God chose the foolish things of the world to shame the wise; God chose the weak things of the world to shame the strong. He chose the lowly things of this world and the despised things—and the things that are not—to nullify the things that are, so that no one may boast before him" (NIV).

God often chooses to work through those who have slipped through the cracks of respectable society. God sees intrinsic value and potential in every human life. We can be too good for God to use but never too bad; too rich but never too poor. As we open our hearts to Him, He creates something beautiful through which He alone is glorified. He plans for us to be His masterpieces of grace.

The true way to be humble is not to stoop until you are smaller than yourself, but to stand at your full height against some higher nature that will show you what the real smallness of your greatness is.

— Philip Brooks

The snow was falling heavily as I rode with a van full of young people on our way to a youth retreat. Nearing our destination, I began to feel a little queasy. I wondered if I had eaten something that had upset my stomach or if I was getting the flu. Arriving at the camp facilities, I was dismayed to discover there were only two washrooms for 100 young people and leaders: one for men and one for women. After what seemed an endless wait, it was finally my turn to use the comfort station—with only minutes to spare before the service began, and just in time to heave my supper.

Still feeling somewhat ill, I mentioned to the pastor, who was leading the meeting, that I was struggling with an upset stomach so he should be prepared in case I had to make a hasty exit.

I had carefully made mental note of a door directly behind the pulpit, which led outside to a snowbank. As I stood to speak, I suddenly knew I would have to make use of that door—in a hurry! Excusing myself rapidly, telling the pastor that I would shortly return, I bee-lined for the door. Once outside, I upchucked the remainder of my supper into the snowbank. A man, who instantly became my immortal hero, arrived with a glass of water and a box of Kleenex.

Still feeling rather green, I re-entered the building. By clinging to the pulpit, I managed to preach to the young people. Some responded to give their lives to Christ. As they continued in prayer, I made another rendezvous with the snowbank.

That episode was a powerful reminder that God did not depend on my eloquence or energy to accomplish His ultimate work. In spite of my utter weakness, His Spirit and power touched hearts and transformed lives.

When David was running from King Saul, a number of men joined his band. Many came with problems, debts, and unresolved conflicts—in some ways they were society's castaways. As they joined David, the Lord worked in them and molded them into a powerful team. Some of them were later listed as the mightiest men in David's army.

It is amazing how often God chooses those whom society passes by—the rejected, the broken, the uneducated, and the plain. With His amazing grace, He makes them usable in His service.

Too many people overvalue what they are not and undervalue what they are.

— Malcolm S. Forbes

On one occasion, I was speaking in a church in Finland, being translated from English by two interpreters into Swedish and Finnish. The three of us were standing on a very small platform, which was covered with a type of rag rug. At the end of the service many people came forward for prayer and pressed close to the front near the two-step high platform.

As I began to reach down to pray with some individuals, the heel of my shoe caught in that ragged carpet and I promptly stumbled, falling flat on the floor at the bottom of the steps. I blushed and bounced upright like a rubber ball. I was hoping against all hope that no one had seen the misstep.

Both translators were horrified. Staring at me owl-eyed, in unison they asked if I was all right. With flaming face, I bounded up the steps and whispered to them to just act as if nothing had happened.

As soon as the service was dismissed I moved quickly to the rear of the building. An elderly friend was seated there. Still feeling quite mortified for the accidental acrobatics, I asked him rather casually if he had seen me fall. He replied, "Oh yes, everybody saw you fall," then reassuringly confided, "but the power of the Lord was so strong, we just thought you couldn't stand!" I wasn't about to give any further explanation.

The scripture says in 2 Corinthians 12:10,

"...for Christ's sake, I delight in weaknesses...in difficulties. For when I am weak, then I am strong" (NIV).

In the moments when our human limitations seem to render us totally ineffective for Christ, or even for ourselves, the power of God in us can make the difference.

In Psalm 121, David talks about lifting up his eyes to the hills, seeking help. He could say this because he was describing a valley experience. In the valleys of life we may sense that we are closed in. Despair can begin to overwhelm us and the immensity of our problem grows higher each hour.

In those moments, we can remember what David said in verse 2:

"*My help cometh from the Lord, which made heaven and earth.*"

Above our difficulties, higher than the mountains, God reigns. He is still in control. His sovereignty is supreme. He will hold us in His precious hands.

The soul would have no rainbow had the eyes no tears.

— John Vance Cheney

The pastor had graciously driven me to the post office in a Paris suburb. At about three o'clock in the afternoon, while we slowly exited the parking lot, four young men casually sauntered in front of the car. The pastor stopped to let them walk past. Suddenly, unexpectedly, they lunged at the car—two pulling open the pastor's door and the other two jerking my door open. I instinctively knew what they wanted.

I had seen these same young men inside the post office a few moments before. They had heard me speaking English and probably assumed I was a rich tourist. When I had returned to the car, I was holding my wallet on my lap—a detail marked by criminal minds.

As his long, sticky fingers closed around my wallet, I hung on with all my might—but it was slipping, slipping. I'm not sure if it was his hand, my hand, or the wallet that hit me under the eye, producing a glorious black and green shiner. Then they were gone—sticky fingers, thieves, and my wallet.

Too stunned to be sensible, I gave chase. Happily for them—and me—I did not catch them. Actually, I didn't want to capture them; I was vainly hoping that they would throw things out of the wallet as they fled, particularly my passport!

After spending several hours at the police station, and at the hospital checking the bruises, I managed to get across the city just in time to preach at the service where I was scheduled to be. The brilliant black eye was an eloquent explanation for my late arrival, as well as an excellent conversation piece.

All night long I relived the scene in my mind, with my emotions fluctuating from anger to anxiety, then to relief. I concluded that I had a multitude of blessings for which to be thankful. The thieves had not harmed us, nor stolen the car (with my suitcase and other valuables in the trunk), and they got very little money for their trouble. With the help of the local pastor, within forty-eight hours I had a replacement passport.

In a moment of crisis we may be overwhelmed, but with hope in Christ, we can walk through each experience. Andrae Crouch sings in his song, *Through it All*: "For if I'd never had a problem, I wouldn't know that God could solve them; I'd never know what faith in God could do." It is through the difficulties that we discover God's sufficient grace.

The book of Exodus gives details of the miraculous deliverance of the Israelites out of Egypt. Nine previous plagues sent by God had already devastated the nation of Egypt. However, when the firstborn died in the final plague, the Bible says that the Israelites were told to leave—in a hurry. At last they were free.

In one night, the entire nation of Israel packed up and marched out of Egypt. There were an estimated 600,000 men, plus women, children, and huge herds of various animals. One can hardly imagine the tremendous organization necessary to set in motion nearly two million people. But God did it, and did it well (Exodus 12:29 to 42).

The Bible gives powerful examples of God manifesting Himself through supernatural provision. He provided for Noah and the animals while they were sheltered in the ark for more than a year. Ravens fed the prophet Elijah. The widow's ever-increasing oil and meal sustained her for several years during a severe drought. Jesus multiplied a handful of buns and a few small fish to feed multitudes—not once, but twice!

When we hold up our impossibilities and inadequacies in the light of God's unlimited resources and abilities, we recognize He is indeed Jehovah-jireh—the All-Sufficient One. Our problems are insignificant in the light of His Sufficiency.

He who has God and everything has no more than he who has God alone.

— C. S. Lewis

There have been a number of occasions when I have experienced God's supernatural provision. I specifically remember one instance when I was ministering in the west of Canada. A few months before, I had made several important and necessary purchases that had completely depleted my financial resources. I had been invited to speak in a number of locations while on my way to minister in the Yukon. Although it was a very long journey, I felt confident that the Lord was directing my way.

I had determined not to make my needs known to anyone, but rather to commit my concerns to the Lord in prayer. I was far from home, with very little money in hand. The Lord blessed the services wonderfully with many young people powerfully challenged to follow Jesus. However, it was a small group and nothing at all was said about reimbursement for expenses.

While packing my bags and loading the car, I knew that I did not have enough cash to purchase gas to get to the next location. That was in the days before credit cards! I waved my goodbyes and turned the car around. I was ready to roll—but with certain angst about how I would get where I was going.

As I turned to wave again, a young man came running across the yard motioning for me to stop. The youth pushed his head into my car. Partly embarrassed, partly apologetic, he shoved an envelope into my hand, "I know you don't need this, but ever since you arrived some days ago, I felt impressed to give it to you," he stammered.

I stared at him wide-eyed for a moment—then thanked him profusely for his obedience to follow God's leading. I also assured him his gift was profoundly appreciated. As I drove down the road, curiosity conquered. I wondered what this teenager had put into the envelope. To my astonishment, I found two crisp new $100-bills. I nearly drove into the ditch! My heart sobbed out my gratitude to the Lord for His faithfulness. It was more than enough to meet the need; the Lord had answered my prayer with abundance.

In the distance we could hear the thunderous roar of the mighty Niagara Falls. As we approached, the air was heavy with vapour rising from the turbulence. Peering down through the cloud of mist we could see the savage rocks seemingly hundreds of meters below us. We stood in awe beside this remarkable landmark of God's handiwork.

Millions of liters of water continuously fall from the ever-flowing river. For thousands of years, night and day, winter and summer, the flow has never ceased. There is always more to come. That is a picture of God's love, His grace and His mercy—ever flowing, without end and with more to follow.

God's work, done in God's way,
will never lack God's supply.
— *Hudson Taylor*

With restrictions regarding luggage varying internationally, I had carefully planned my tour with minimum necessities in my suitcase. After arriving, someone mentioned that while I was travelling within Europe I was only permitted twenty kilos of baggage. I was horrified and immediately began to think of what possessions in my suitcase I could possibly live without.

With thoughts of high-cost penalties in mind, I paid a small fortune to mail a package of items to friends in the next location where it could wait for my arrival. I gave away a precious chocolate bar that I had stowed. I was still way over the limit.

Frantically, I telephoned to inquire how much I would be charged for the overweight baggage. The agent told me to inspect my ticket and asked me if it had been purchased in Canada. He inquired if the ticket specified the amount of luggage. That's when I noticed the little code that signalled, "Two pieces allowed." My limit was not twenty kilos, but forty-six kilos!

It was too late to recover my precious chocolate bar or the expensive package that had already been mailed. It would have been possible to freely transport it all and more. The provisions had been included in the ticket.

How many times we shudder and tremble with despair, barely daring to ask for help and blessing from the Lord. All the time, His abundant provision of mercy and grace is more than enough—fully supplied and paid for at the cross. In Hebrews 4:16 we have this invitation:

"Let us therefore come boldly unto the throne of grace, that we may obtain mercy, and find grace to help in time of need."

One evening when I was feeling overwhelmed with a sense of inadequacy in face of a particular need, the Lord used the promise of 2 Corinthians 9:8 to renew my hope in His grace. It says:

"And God is able to make all grace abound to you, so that in all things at all times, having all that you need, you will abound in every good work" (NIV).

God, as He is revealed in the Bible, is full of tender mercy and amazing grace. In our experience we also discover His faithfulness, compassion, and unconditional love. The wonder is not only His care for us but also the impartation of His Spirit within, allowing us to be His hands extended to others. He desires to brush the tears from broken hearts—through us.

The only ones among you who will be really happy are those who will have sought and found how to serve.

— Albert Schweitzer

The problems of Northern Ireland are complicated and tragic. During the "troubles" that lasted nearly thirty years, hundreds of people were caught in the crossfire on both sides of the conflict.

A country church called Mountain Lodge was located almost on the border of Southern Ireland near the town of Darkley, Northern Ireland. It was in a deeply troubled area filled with violence. The believers who were members of this assembly were known to be neutral and had not been particularly targeted. That was about to change. On November 20, 1983, the evening service was just beginning. Folks were gathering and the musicians were playing introductory hymns.

Suddenly, masked gunmen burst through the door, shooting at everyone in sight, in the foyer as well as in the sanctuary. More than seventy rounds of ammunition poured into the building. Three men were left dead and many wounded. The horror of the unprovoked attack against innocent civilians made international headlines.

Twenty-four years later, it was a great honor for me to minister in this assembly. To witness God's grace in bringing healing to those who had experienced that nightmare was amazing. More remarkable is the ministry outreach the assembly continues to offer to all the surrounding communities—bringing hope, reconciliation, and forgiveness. The profoundness of the gospel of Christ is revealed when God's grace empowers His people to rise from the ashes of tragedy and walk on in His peace—living and giving God's love to others.

Chapter Seven

OVERCOMING BY OBEDIENCE

One of the most important life-lessons we can learn is to be responsible for our choices. We are never tempted by what we don't like. We do not fall into temptation, we *dive* into it. Today we *are* the result of the choices we made yesterday; tomorrow we will be the result of the decisions we make today.

We must recognize the peril of un-confronted sin. The voice of the conscience always speaks for God—it always takes God's side. Quickly, we must yield and abandon our rights to the Lordship of Jesus. In surrender we find the amazing empowerment of Christ, which makes us more than conquerors.

In Genesis 32:27 and 28, the angel who was wresting with Jacob asked him, "...*What is thy name? And he said, Jacob. And he said, Thy name shall be called no more Jacob, but Israel: for as a prince hast thou power with God and with men, and hast prevailed.*"

Names in Bible times carried tremendous significance. The name *Jacob* in Hebrew means *deceiver*. He had lived up to that name very well. Taking advantage of his blind father, he pretended to be his brother Esau and claimed the birthright blessing. Esau was furious; Jacob fled for his life.

Later, as he was returning from his exile, he was confronted with his failures and faced possible death at the hand of his angry brother. At that moment of dilemma, the Angel of the Lord appeared to him and they wrestled. At the Angel's insistence, he admitted his name was Jacob, the deceiver. When he owned up to who he had become, immediately the Angel of the Lord changed his name to Israel, which means *prince with God*.

When we face our sin, taking responsibility for who we are, God's power is released to change us. Jesus told of the man who found complete forgiveness with a simple prayer: "Lord be merciful to me, a sinner."

I believe that we are solely responsible for our choices, and we have to accept the consequences of every deed, word, and thought throughout our lifetime.

— Elizabeth Kubler-Ross

We had just finished a delicious meal and a beautiful carrot cake was brought on for dessert. Although I was tempted to indulge, I resisted, taking only one small piece. The next evening, I had reserved space for another taste of the delicious treat. In fact, my mouth was watering with anticipation.

With a puzzled expression, the hostess returned to the table and queried her husband, "Where is the cake?" It was a moment of truth. He hadn't intended to, but with little snacks here and nibbles there, he admitted he had eaten *the whole cake!*

This incident reminded me of another friend who had made several scrumptious blueberry pies. She had covered them with a tea towel and set them on the kitchen counter to cool, warning her three-year-old son not to touch them.

When she came in from the garden a few minutes later, she noticed a blueberry-covered spoon in the sink. The pies had been neatly re-covered and the culprit's get-away chair had been pushed back to the table. Upon investigation, however, she discovered that a hole had been eaten out of the center of each pie. One look at her son's blueberry-tinted face and she knew exactly who was guilty. Upon her accusation, the boy's eyes grew large with awe, and he exclaimed, "Moms know everything!"

We may feel that the little nibbles of sin—a taste here, a look there—will be unnoticed by the Lord. But He knows what we are up to; He is omniscient. The Bible asserts: *"Be sure your sin will find you out"* (Numbers 32:23). He calls us to repentance and reconciliation.

In Psalm 73, Asaph confesses disappointment because it appeared the wicked were prospering while he was experiencing great difficulties. He describes his inner struggle with what seemed so unfair. But in verses 17 and 18 he has an encounter with God that illuminates the eternal perspective:

"*...then I understood their final destiny. Surely you place them on slippery ground; you cast them down to ruin*" (NIV).

We must never be envious of the apparent successes of those who are corrupt and arrogant. Without Christ, their end is unspeakable disaster. Let us always consider success in the light of eternal values. Without Christ, life is nothing but vanity and vapour; with Christ, we have everything we need for this world and the world to come.

Never esteem anything as an advantage to you that will make you break your word or lose your self-respect.

— Marcus Aurelius

My friend carefully put the lure on the fishhook and handed me the rod. Following his instructions, I lowered the line into the water, peering over the edge of the boat into the clear mountain lake. I could see the fish swimming about as the bait slowly descended past them. Some came for a closer look; some actually gently nudged it while other fish turned tail and swam away. I jiggled the line ever so slightly. Trying to entice a fish was serious business—to make them hungry or curious enough to take the bait.

Sure enough, from the sidelines an innocent fish was attracted by the lure. With a sudden swoop it caught the bait but, alas, it also caught my hidden hook. Too late it tried to flee; above I whooped with glee! He fought in vain as I slowly, steadily reeled in the line. His fate was sealed. The supper was delicious.

Playing the tempter instead of being the tempted gave another dimension to this whole affair of life. I was amazed at the parallels. The enemy of our soul exerts every effort to distract us. He has a wide array of tasty morsels. He carefully hides the hooks with which he would control and destroy. When we fall for his wiles and bite his bait, the line becomes taut; we find ourselves held fast and heading in a direction we didn't foresee.

God has not left us without His help. James 4:7 proclaims:

"Submit yourselves, then, to God. Resist the devil, and he will flee from you" (NIV).

In 1 Kings chapter 8, we read the prayer of Solomon at the dedication of the temple in Jerusalem. Knowing that the Israelites may stray away from God, with earnest supplication Solomon requests that the Lord intervene with deliverance if they repent and call for God's mercy. How often, however, the people of Israel suffered anguish because they simply would not return to the Lord with repentance.

The importance and power of repentance has never changed. It determines our eternal destiny—heaven or hell. Jesus said so in Luke 13:3. The Amplified Version puts it this way:

"...unless you repent (change your mind for the better and heartily amend your ways, with abhorrence of your past sins), you will all likewise perish and be lost eternally."

Although society endorses sin and evil, even mocking its gravity, we must never underestimate the necessity of heart repentance. With our hearts ever tender, let us be quick to turn from our sinful ways—asking for and receiving forgiveness from God.

You don't get to choose how you are going to die. Or when. You can only decide how you are going to live, now.

— Joan Baez

The story of Zacchaeus in Luke 19:1 to 10 describes how this wicked, but vertically challenged tax collector wants to see Jesus. He realizes that if he could climb into a tree he would have an excellent vantage point without being hassled by the crowds. When Jesus comes directly under the tree, however, he looks up and sees Zacchaeus perched on a branch. He invites him to come down to receive forgiveness and transformation.

I was deeply engrossed in my message while using this story to explain how the power of Christ could change the human heart. Suddenly, I espied a three-meter decorative tree on the side of the platform. I had a perfect prop to illustrate my point. Dashing to the tree, I pulled aside its branches and addressed the crowd through the plastic leaves.

I had failed to realize, however, that no one had climbed into that tree in recent times. There was a heavy accumulation of dust and cobwebs. As I spoke, the clouds of dust made me sneeze—creating huge billows of grey powder. Stepping out of the tree, I realized my clothes had changed color. It actually appeared as though I had fallen into a flour bin, my face faintly resembling a racoon's. I was somewhat perturbed—but the audience was in hysterics!

Eventually, we all have to come out of the bushes where we try to hide. Like Adam in the Garden of Eden, God knows where we are. The specks of sin contaminate our best appearances and it is clear to all where we have been. But the power of the Gospel can bring purification, transformation, and liberation.

Even when Jesus plainly told the disciples in Matthew 20:18 and 19 that He would go to Jerusalem to be arrested, whipped, crucified, and then raised from the dead, they did not seem to hear a word He said. Can we also sometimes be so deaf and blind? Could there be occasions when the Holy Spirit calls, warns and cajoles, but we do not hear?

Through the Word of God and the circumstances of life, the Lord may be calling us. If His quiet voice within is urging us to specific action, we will only find release in obedience.

*Though no one can go back
and make a brand new start,
anyone can start from now
and make a brand new ending.*

— Carl Bard

As a pre-schooler, being several years younger than my three siblings and being more than a little spoiled, I had become an extremely fussy eater. Mealtime revolved around my whining and my family's wheedling as they vainly tried to get me to eat. On occasion, one of my father's hired men would join us for dinner. He was a large-framed man with a rather gruff voice and rough bearing. He would quietly watch these episodes—which would generally leave everyone exhausted and me smugly getting my own way.

One day, as I was throwing my typical tantrum, he suddenly stood up, leaned his huge frame across the table into my face, and firmly articulated, "Eat!" The sight of this gigantic man's shaggy head inches from mine and the sound of his rumbling voice had an immediate effect. I made an instant choice. I shoveled food onto my spoon and gulped every crumb from my plate. My mother always chuckled as, from that day onward, she related how I was never a picky eater.

There are moments when all cajoling fails and confrontation is necessary. The root of problems can be dealt with; we can see change produced in our lives.

The Lord revealed Himself in a powerful vision to Isaiah. In chapter 6, the prophet describes the awesome glory of God on His throne, surrounded by the adoring angels acclaiming His holiness. In the presence of the Lord, he became acutely aware of his own unworthiness and deep need for mercy and cleansing from sin. In Isaiah 6:5, he cries out:

"...Woe is me! for I am undone; because I am a man of unclean lips, and I dwell in the midst of a people of unclean lips: for mine eyes have seen the King, the LORD of hosts."

As we draw ever closer to the Lord, we also discover the depths of our need and the greatness of God's grace. God had an answer for Isaiah in his despair, shame, and guilt. The following verse declares that the angel touched him and Isaiah was changed. The fire of God transformed him. As we recognize our need and call out to the Lord, He is faithful to forgive, sustain, and deliver us. Let us also cry out like Isaiah for His mercy and then in utter surrender, submit to His will.

It's easier to fight for one's principles than to live up to them.

— Alfred Adler

As the train twisted through the tortuous mountain terrain, I was filled with wonder as I stared out the window. The pouring rain of the last few days in the Swiss Alps had filled the canyons. Everywhere waterfalls cascaded down the mountains and rushed through the gullies below. The train slowly crossed deep ravines on narrow bridges above churning rivers, passing through the heavy cloud and steady rain. It was awe-inspiring—until the train stopped!

Two mudslides along the track ahead meant that we all had to disembark at the little mountain station and transfer to a waiting bus. Not a problem, except that the rain, which had looked so beautiful through the train window, was now pouring down on my head!

After walking the short distance to the bus, then to another train a little while later, I was totally drenched, uncomfortable, and looked like a half-drowned rat. The scenery had somehow changed. Now my focus was on the steady drip of water down my neck. My friend dryly commented that it was a good thing the mudslide had not come down on the train. Of course there is always something for which to be thankful!

Without water, we cannot live. Controlled and canalized, it brings life to the earth. Out of control it can become one of the most destructive natural forces; it can wreak havoc, destruction, pain, and death.

So it is with the passions of life. Without the control of the Holy Spirit, the necessary desires of humanity can destroy the soul, bringing pain and spiritual death. The principles of God's Word, which teach moral absolutes, are meant to channel human behavior and bring life and blessing. The seductive forces of darkness that emphasize instant and selfish gratification, unleash destruction and pain. As we surrender to Christ, His power and forgiveness can transform tumult and destruction into beauty and blessing.

I have been deeply challenged by the words of Matthew 7:21, where Jesus gives this strong warning:

"Not every one that saith unto me, Lord, Lord, shall enter into the kingdom of heaven; but he that doeth the will of my Father who is in heaven" (ASV).

Following this admonition, Jesus spoke of the house built on the rock versus the house built on the sand. Jesus made it clear that both builders had heard His words. However, those who built on the Rock obeyed them. It is not enough just to hear God's Word; we must apply the principles and live out His commands by the grace of God.

*Right is right, even if everyone is against it,
and wrong is wrong,
even if everyone is for it.*
— William Penn

Driving the convoluted roads of Europe is a challenge. The narrow and horrendously crowded city streets are nerve-wracking. My friend owns a Global Positioning System. It is truly a marvellous and useful invention. With pin-point accuracy, the computerized woman's voice told us where to go and how to get there. In pouring rain, dense fog, or brilliant sunshine, she knew the road and continually reminded us of the direction to take.

There were moments, however, when she could really get under our skin. Her cheerful, "You are going faster than the speed limit," could be downright irritating. She did not say it just once, but continued to do so at every possible opportunity. If we made a wrong turn, she insistently expressed displeasure by telling us to turn around as soon as possible. We also noticed if we ignored her long enough, our ears tuned her out; her admonishing was to no avail.

There are a number of parallels between her cautioning and the conscience—that interior voice that can be a compass for the soul. When we surrender our lives to Christ, the conscience is awakened to hear the voice of God. Persistently He speaks, directing, calling, and drawing us ever closer to Himself. We can, however, choose to ignore His words. Soon the calls to change direction, slow down, or go His way are buried, unheard beneath the busy-ness of doing our own thing.

The secret of silencing the computerized woman's reproof, or the far more serious consequence of healing our bruised conscience, is obedience. When we submit to God's will, His peace instantly fills our hearts.

Often, we are deeply troubled by the immorality promoted in our society. We compare the moral situation to Sodom. However, the root of the sin of Sodom touches us much more personally when we read Ezekiel 16:49 and 50:

"Behold, this was the iniquity of thy sister Sodom, pride, fullness of bread, and abundance of idleness was in her and in her daughters, neither did she strengthen the hand of the poor and needy. And they were haughty, and committed abomination before me: therefore I took them away as I saw good."

The root of her moral sin was imbedded in pride, self-gratification, and *"prosperous ease"* (ASV). Those roots are subtle and dangerous. We must trust in the blood of Christ to cleanse us daily, continually guarding us against these deadly inward attitudes from which spring the outward manifestations of depravity.

Repentance is being so sorry for sin you quit sinning.
— Author Unknown

My friend was jubilant. While shopping that morning she had bought two pairs of stylish shoes on sale for half price. I watched carefully to see how she would convince her husband of the excellence of her purchase. Some hours later, as we were eating a lovely meal together, she mentioned her new shoes to him, particularly emphasizing the sale price. Then she showed them to him. He could say little because his mouth was full of pork chop.

She carefully arranged them on the floor beside his chair. With a wink to me, she suggested that she would just leave them there so he could get accustomed to them. As soon as the dinner was finished, she put them on and modelled their elegance for him. He was now full of delicious pork chops. Having had a half hour to admire the shoes from a distance, he capitulated without complaint.

Besides learning an amusing secret of marital bliss, I was transfixed by the parallel of more sinister temptations in human experience. The enemy carefully plots our weak moments, taking advantage of our tolerance until our conscience becomes complacent.

As we become accustomed to an environment of sin, it is only a step until we are sufficiently desensitized to participate in it. A warning of this sequence of descent is clearly described in Psalm 1:1:

"Blessed is the man who does not walk in the counsel of the wicked or stand in the way of sinners or sit in the seat of mockers" (NIV).

Chapter Eight

DETERMINING DESTINY

Jesus makes the bold declaration in John 14:6: "*...I am the Way, the Truth, and the Life: no man cometh unto the Father, but by me.*"

He has given us the path, the purpose, and the power to walk in a living relationship with God. When we choose to acknowledge our need of God, repent of our sin, and submit our will to Jesus Christ, we are born from above into the Kingdom of God. To reject His voice calling us to follow Him is to walk on without God and without hope. The broad road of selfishness and sin leads to the sure destiny of eternal destruction.

One stanza of the beloved hymn, *Amazing Grace,* written by John Newton, sums up well our walk with Christ and our hope in Him:

Through many dangers toils and snares,
I have already come,
'Tis Grace has brought me safe thus far
And grace will lead me home.

The Apostle Paul states in Romans 1:16:

"*For I am not ashamed of the gospel of Christ: for it is the power of God unto salvation to everyone that believeth....*"

There is nothing in the world comparable to the good news that we can find forgiveness and peace with God through the death and resurrection of Christ.

Within the human heart there is an intense void. It has been described as a "God-sized vacancy". People have tried to fill this emptiness with money, materialism, relationships, and pleasures—all to no avail. The place has been created by God and for Him alone. Nothing less will satisfy.

Paul declared relationship with God through Jesus Christ as the only gospel that has the power to transform lives, bringing fulfillment and eternal hope. We have the opportunity to reject or accept this life-changing message by faith.

Brethren, be great believers.
Little faith will bring your souls to heaven,
but great faith will bring heaven to your souls.
— Charles Spurgeon

A morning walk is invigorating. While staying at a hotel in an unfamiliar city, I asked directions to the nearest walking path. The clerk drew a quick map, outlining the area, and pointed me in the general direction.

As I started down the road, I couldn't identify where I was on her map so I asked a passerby. She had never heard of the footpath. As I continued walking, I met another woman who said she had heard of it, but had no idea where it was. Soon I saw a man mowing his lawn. He assured me I was going in the right direction and if I would continue, sooner or later I would find it. Shortly afterward, a lady approached pushing her little girl in a stroller. While waving her arms in all directions, she informed me that, although she had never been there, she had heard it was a beautiful place to walk.

By then I had been walking for fifteen minutes. A jogger bounced past me. Before I had time to ask him where I was, he smiled, waved, and disappeared down the street. I slowed my pace. Where exactly was I? Where was I going? By this time, I was not even sure where I had come from! Another woman approached. She cheerfully responded to my query.

"Follow me, I'm going there myself," she said.

How grateful I was at last to find someone who could and would show me the way. Later, as I reflected on the experience, I realized that countless people don't know where they are or where they are going in life. They are searching for meaning, for destiny. They are probing for purpose. When asked, others can give no answers for they don't know where they are going themselves. Some are too busy. Others have heard there is help and hope, but having never received themselves, they are unable to direct anyone else.

Thank God, His Word makes it possible to receive clear direction throughout life. It is my desire not only to point people to the right path but also to walk with them as we journey together, following Christ.

The Book of Ecclesiastes tells of Solomon's search through every available activity, including education, business ventures, and selfish indulgence. He set his heart on finding meaning in life—not unlike a great number of people today. His search led him down innumerable dead-end rabbit trails. In Ecclesiastes 12:13 and 14 we read of his great discovery:

"Let us hear the conclusion of the whole matter: Fear God, and keep his commandments: for this is the whole duty of man. For God shall bring every work into judgment, with every secret thing, whether it be good, or whether it be evil."

In our frantic lifestyles, it is vitally important for us to appreciate this most valuable and precious lesson. Unlike Solomon, we don't have to learn the hard way. We can take God at His Word and apply the same principles that Jesus taught.

Many persons have the wrong idea
of what constitutes true happiness.
It is not attained through self-gratification,
but through fidelity to a worthy purpose.
— Helen Keller

As I left the home where I was staying, I followed the street, walking straight ahead. Having passed several intersections, I came to a junction where I had to choose to continue to the left or the right. On the right side, I noticed a large white memorial cross.

I continued walking for nearly an hour. As I returned, I became somewhat confused because of all the roads I had passed. I began to feel a little ridiculous, being sure I was quite lost. Then I saw the cross. I knew that when I found the cross, I could easily find my way home.

The Bible makes it clear that we have lost our way on the road of life (Isaiah 53:6). Alone, lost, and not knowing where to turn, we walk on in the hopelessness of life separated from God. But there is a sure signpost pointing the way: the Cross of Christ.

The Word of God teaches that if we will recognize our lost estate and call for mercy to the One who gave His life for our salvation, we can begin to walk in The Way. Come to the cross; find your way home from there.

As Jesus was explaining that He was the living water and the bread of life, He indicated that many would not believe. In John 6:37, however, a wonderful promise is given:

"All that the Father giveth me shall come to me; and him that cometh to me I will in no wise cast out."

When the Holy Spirit convicts us of our sin, we are being drawn by God into relationship with Him. As we surrender to Him, His arms are open to receive us, to change us. He will never turn away a seeking, surrendering heart.

The tragedy of life is not that it ends so soon, but that we wait so long to begin it.

— Author Unknown

It became apparent that another computer would be helpful in the office. Not being particularly adept at surfing the Internet, I asked my secretary to see if she could find what we wanted by bidding on eBay. Very shortly, she enthusiastically informed me that she had made a bid on an ideal product. Later, somewhat crestfallen, she admitted that she had missed catching the bargain.

"I was a dollar short and a minute late," she conceded.

Pondering these words caused me to reflect on the more serious message. There are people who carelessly live life, never considering eternal consequences. Perhaps they are thinking that at some point they will make a bid for hope by claiming the credits of a good work.

The Word of God clearly teaches that our hope is not in our own goodness but in God's grace and forgiveness when we cast ourselves upon His mercy. We have nothing to claim but the promise of Christ and His work accomplished for us on the cross.

What a tragedy to think of those who hope to earn eternal life by their own merits. How dreadful for them to discover—too late—the utter worthlessness and inability of human efforts. How sobering and serious to reflect on the possibility of standing before the Judge of the earth at the end of time and hearing Him pronounce, "Too late."

Amid the wickedness of his generation, Noah caught the attention of the Lord. God made provision to sustain this righteous man. In Genesis 6:8, we read: "...*Noah found grace in the eyes of the LORD.*" God had His eye on him. In the conflicts of good versus evil, God sees and knows those who seek after Him.

Science has no way to define the cause or conflict of conscience. Even those who refuse to acknowledge God's involvement in human affairs are at a total loss to explain this universal voice—the moral code. Crossing all cultures and languages, the basic principles of love, fairness, and freedom are clearly understood.

The conscience is the voice of God speaking within the heart of every person. We have the power to choose right or wrong, good or evil. Our choices have eternal consequences. The Bible clearly states in Romans 6:23:

"*For the wages of sin is death; but the gift of God is eternal life through Jesus Christ our Lord.*"

Our eternal destiny is determined by our acceptance or rejection of God's provision of salvation through Jesus Christ.

The only person you are destined to become is the person you decide to be.
— Ralph Waldo Emerson

Some friends live in a typical mountain village in Switzerland. Perched precariously on a narrow slice of land, the chalets border a steep ravine several hundred meters deep. I was informed that a huge hydroelectric dam was situated about eight kilometers up the ravine, creating electricity for the region. I was also informed that a warning siren had been installed in the attic of the house where I was lodging. If the dam broke, the siren would sound, warning everyone in the village to escape.

It was not the water rushing from the dam that would be the danger, but rather the air vacuum created by the sudden surge of released water. Apparently it would suck all the houses clinging to the cliffs into the canyon. The villagers would have only minutes in which to flee.

I thought it might be a good idea to keep my shoes and coat near the bed when I went to sleep that night, although I never did find out where we were supposed to go when we escaped. The puzzle to me was why anyone would choose to live in such a perilous location in the first place. Something of human nature longs to defy the impossible, I suppose.

Those who live without respect for God's Word and build their lives without regard for Him are in a far more hazardous position. All may go well for a very long time, but the day will come when whatever is not founded in Him will be swept away. Where shall they escape on that day?

One of the greatest tragedies in the world has to be the regrets of a life misspent. I have encountered people from various walks of life who expressed deep sadness for mistakes of their past. Wrong decisions had produced pain. Dark habits had contaminated lifestyles. Wasted time and talent was forever lost. Golden opportunities now lay buried beneath the words, "If only..."

A prayer of Moses, recorded in Psalm 90:2, provides excellent advice:

"Teach us to number our days aright, that we may gain a heart of wisdom" (NIV).

During the brief days we have on this earth we must apply our hearts to living life with eternity in view. In James 4:14 we are reminded:

"What is your life? You are a mist that appears for a little while and then vanishes" (NIV).

The Bible shows the way to peace with God through Jesus Christ. Our purpose becomes clear. We live our lives to bring glory to God and goodwill to our fellow man. When Jesus Christ is our reason for living, eternal values become our priority. There are no regrets for the one who walks with God.

For all sad words of tongue or pen the saddest are these: "It might have been."

— John Greenleaf Whittier

The fairytale is told of an ancient king who summoned his court jester. He requested the clown to travel throughout the kingdom in search of a fool greater than the jester himself. When one was found, he was to bestow upon him the identity of greatest fool in the kingdom.

For many months the jester journeyed, asking questions of everyone as he searched for one foolish enough to deserve the new title. Unsuccessful, at last he returned to find his king weak, sickly, and near death. In the audience of his king, however, he asked the same questions: "Where are you going? Have you prepared for the journey?"

The king replied, "I don't know where I am going, and have made no preparation."

The jester announced, "You, my king, are the greatest fool I have found in the kingdom."

Although this story may seem unusual, it packs a powerful truth. For many who live in our fast-paced, selfish society, life rushes by with never a thought of eternity.

Some attempt to drown pain and fear of death with addictions, vices, or feverish activity. Others, who realize their time is short, fill their last weeks with frantic effort to gain a few more days—even hours—of life. There are those who ignore completely the spiritual thirst of their souls. Few, indeed, take the time to prepare to meet God. In the light of eternity, however, there is nothing of greater importance.

We shall all meet God. The Bible clearly states the fact in Hebrews 9:27: "...it is appointed unto men once to die, but after this the judgment." The great question is, are we ready for this encounter?

The wonderful news of the Gospel is that it is possible to have peace with God and experience the assurance of eternal life. The cross of Jesus provides pardon for sin; repentance brings forgiveness. His indwelling presence gives assurance of eternal hope. Make your peace with God now.

One of the most precious promises about the believer's eternal destiny was spoken by Jesus in John 14:1 to 3:

"Let not your heart be troubled: ye believe in God, believe also in me. In my Father's house are many mansions: if it were not so, I would have told you. I go to prepare a place for you. And if I go and prepare a place for you, I will come again, and receive you unto myself; that where I am, there ye may be also."

Michael Faraday, who was considered to have been one of the greatest experimental physicists, was questioned on his speculation on life after death. He answered, "Speculation? I know nothing about speculations. I'm resting on certainties. I know that my Redeemer lives, and because He lives, I shall live also."

When Christ calls me home I shall go with the gladness of a boy bounding away from school.
— Adoniram Judson
(first Christian missionary to Burma)

My mother lived her life with radiant faith in God. One month before her ninety-sixth birthday, she passed away. My friend Janis[1] spent some time with my mother a few hours before she went to be with her Lord. In the following excerpt, Janis recounted what happened during that visit.

"I took her hand in mine and we talked a little about our families. Then, looking toward the foot of her bed she asked me, 'Do you see that man in the white suit?' I told her that I didn't see anyone. A few minutes later she questioned again, 'Did you see that man in the shiny white suit?' I responded that I had not. I queried if he had spoken anything to her. She looked at me and answered, 'He told me that I am going to be moving to a new room soon.'

"I replied, 'Yes, and everything is going to be alright.' I was still holding her hand as she closed her eyes and rested. As I watched her, I wasn't sure what to do. I could pray, but then decided to sing a little song about the peace of God.

"After a few minutes she opened her eyes and said, 'There's an angel standing behind you!' I quickly glanced over my shoulder. I wanted to look, but at the same time I didn't want to. She asked me again if I had seen the angel. I had not, but I knew she had. As we were talking, she casually stated, 'I am going to see Jesus.'"

One day, our journey on earth will be over. The joys, the sorrows, like brief dancing shadows, fleeting, shall be gone. Others may drive our cars, live in our houses, and work at our jobs. The history of our earthly sojourn will gradually fade into the etchings on tombstones.

For those who know Christ, however, the reality of eternal life will have just begun. Forever we will be in the presence of Him who died that we might live.

---

[1] Janis Wessel shared this experience at my mother's funeral and in a letter to the family.

In 2 Corinthians 4:18, we are instructed:

"…look not at the things which are seen, but at the things which are not seen: for the things which are seen are temporal; but the things which are not seen are eternal."

We need to continually re-evaluate our priorities, recognizing that material wealth and pleasure will very soon be gone. All that is in the visible world will eventually be destroyed—by time, rust or rot.

Only the Word of God and the qualifying virtues of faith, hope, and love will endure when we stand before Christ. Therefore, our strength, our purposes, indeed every fiber of our existence, should be built around eternal values—for they alone shall last forever.

Only one life, 'twill soon be past.
Only what's done for Christ will last.
— Author Unknown

I was deeply involved in the heavy schedule, totally concentrated on my plans and preparations when suddenly everything was disrupted. I would have to leave for another place. All my appointments were put on hold and I was forced to turn my heart in a totally different direction.

However, as I neared the new destination, the disappointments and disarray that I had left behind slowly faded from my mind. I began to anticipate the new challenges and blessings awaiting me.

I wonder if our departure from this life will be like that. All the pushing and shoving, the buying and selling, the anxiety and pain will fade from view as our hearts become conscious of His Eternal Kingdom. In that moment, all the vanities of our earthly existence will be but fast-fading memories in the light of His Glory.

Conclusion

A friend, who has three young children, related the account of a family outing they had taken together. As they climbed a steep incline, he carried his ten-month-old daughter and held the hand of his three-year-old son while their five-year-old girl walked beside him and his wife. Each precious child arrived at the top of the hill.

As we travel through life, some of God's children need to be carried; they are unable to walk alone. Others can walk, but desperately need to feel the Father's hand. Some can be trusted to walk in the strength their maturity has provided. However, all need to sense the direction and assurance of the Father's presence.

Life is a journey. Along the road we meet those who mark us forever with a word here or a smile there. Likewise, our footprints will make it easier or more difficult for those who follow us. Gratefulness will turn the rough patches into pleasure and lighten heavy loads. With a clear focus, our purpose and direction are established. Proper priorities are the foundation of enduring vision.

Climbing the rough hills, traversing the dark descents, we press on. Difficulties create endurance and perseverance as we progress. Every night will eventually give way to the morning sun. Although the road becomes long, hope springs with each new opportunity.

Our God has promised all the grace necessary. He is sufficient for every need along the road. As we face the obstacles, pressures, and temptations, we recognize our limitations—our desperate need of divine help and guidance. Through surrender and obedience to Christ, however, we shall safely make it home.

Whatever the path ahead may hold for you, may you walk in a living relationship with Christ. May His presence be your reality—for in His presence you will find fullness of joy in the journey of life.

The Gift of Salvation

If you have never given your life to Christ, I sincerely urge you to surrender to Him today. According to Romans 3:23, "*...all have sinned, and come short of the glory of God.*"

The Bible tells us that peace with God is received by turning to Him from our sins. In Romans 10:9, 10 and 13 we read:

"*...if you confess with your mouth, 'Jesus is Lord,' and believe in your heart that God raised him from the dead, you will be saved. For it is with your heart that you believe and are justified, and it is with your mouth that you confess and are saved. ...for, 'Everyone who calls on the name of the Lord will be saved'*" (NIV).

You can receive His life now by repentance and faith. Pray this simple prayer: "Lord, I know I have sinned. I believe You are the Son of God and that You died on the cross to forgive my sins. I believe You have risen from the dead with power to give me a transformed life. Please forgive me, change my heart, and set me free. I surrender the control of my will to You. Help me to follow You. In Jesus' Name. Amen."

Read the Bible and pray every day. Find others who love Jesus who can help you to follow Him. With your hand in the hand of Jesus, you will finish your journey with joy.

Bibliography and Sources

Books:

Canfield, Jack, *et al. Chicken Soup for the Soul: Stories of Faith*. Cos Cob, CT: Chicken Soup for the Soul Publishing, LLC, 2008.

Mason, John. *Don't Wait for Your Ship to Come In...Swim Out to Meet It*. Tulsa, OK: Honor Books, 1994.

Prochnow, Herbert V., & Prochnow, Herbert V. Jr. *A Dictionary of Wit, Wisdom and Humor*. Grand Rapids, MI: Baker Book House, 1975.

Internet Sources:

Rhyme, *For Want of a Nail*, www.rhymes.org.uk

Adler, Alfred, quote, www.quoteworld.org

Assisi, St. Francis of, prayer, *Channel of Peace*, www.wedding-guideuk.com

Aurelius, Marcus, quote, www.quoteworld.org

Baez, Joan, quote, www.brainyquote.com

Barclay, William, quote, www.thinkexist.com

Bard, Carl, quote, www.thinkexist.com

Bombeck, Erma, quote, www.thinkexist.com

Brooks, Philip, quote, www.giga.usa.com

Cheney, John Vance, quote, www.thinkexist.com

Chesterton, G. K., quote, www.thinkexist.com

Churchill, Winston, quote, www.brainyquote.com

Cicero, Marcus Tullius, quote, www.quoteworld.org

Crouch, Andrae, song, *Through It All*, www.karaoke.goloom.com

Einstein, Albert, quote, www.thinkexist.com

Eisenhower, Dwight D. quote, www.famousquotesandauthors.com

Emerson, Ralph Waldo, quote, www.thinkexist.com

Epicurus, quote, www.quotationsbook.com

Forbes, Malcolm, quote, http://en.wikiquote.org

Frick, James W., quote, www.thinkexist.com

Heinlein, Robert, quote, www.quotationspage.com

Judson, Adoniram, quote, www.wholesomewords.org

Keller, Helen, quote, www.quotationspage.com

Kubler-Ross, Elisabeth, quote, www.thinkexist.com

Kubler-Ross, Elisabeth, quote, www.brainyquote.com

Maxwell, John, quote, www.jesussite.com

Nicholas, David, quote, www.thinkexist.com

Oatman, Johnson, song, *Count Your Blessings*, www.time-lesstruths.org

Penn, William, quote, www.randomterrain.com

Schweitzer, Albert, quote, www.brainyquote.com

Sheen, Bishop Fulton, quote, www.quoteb.com

Spurgeon, Charles Haddon, quote, www.quotationspage.com

Swift, Jonathan, quote, www.shipul.com

Taylor, Hudson, quote, http://home.snu.edu

Whittier, John Greenleaf, quote, www.brainyquote.com

We invite you to visit Anita's Web Site,

www.inspirationministries.net

for more ministry information, and a full listing of available
materials, books and gospel music.

Inspiration Ministries presents these CDs of Country Gospel Music
by Anita Pearce

Grace   Mercy   He Loved
                                                    Me Enough

Each CD is available for $20.

These two books are also available by the same author:

Above the Storm   *Choose to Live Life*
$15.00 $12.00

To order, send cheque or money order, including $5.00 shipping, to:
Inspiration Ministries
Box 44
Margo, SK
Canada S0A 2M0
OR you can order online. All prices are in Canadian funds.